# THE PROLIFIC
# AND THE DEVOURER

# THE
# PROLIFIC
# AND THE
# DEVOURER

W. H. AUDEN

THE ECCO PRESS

THE ECCO PRESS
100 West Broad Street
Hopewell, New Jersey 08525
Published simultaneously in Canada by
Penguin Books Canada Ltd., Ontario
Printed in the United States of America
Designed by Janet Tingey

*Library of Congress Cataloging-in-Publication Data*

Auden, W. H. (Wystan Hugh), 1907–1973.
The prolific and the devourer / W. H. Auden.—1st ed.
p.     cm.
ISBN 0-88001-345-1
ISBN 0-88001-465-2 (paperback)
1. Aphorisms and apothegms. I. Title.
PR6001.U4P76    1993
818'.5202—dc20    93-2409
CIP
r93

The text of this book is set in Garamond Number 3.

9  8  7  6  5  4  3  2  1

FIRST ECCO PAPERBACK EDITION

# CONTENTS

# PREFACE
## by Edward Mendelson

_____

*The Prolific and the Devourer* is a book of aphorisms and reflections that Auden wrote in the spring and summer— and abandoned in the autumn—of 1939. It displays Auden's attitudes in his first months in America, at a moment of transition between his equivocal Marxism in the 1930s and his committed Christianity in the 1940s and after.

Around May 1939, in a letter to Mrs. A. E. Dodds, an Oxford friend and wife of E. R. Dodds, Auden said of the book: "it is just a new Marriage of Heaven and Hell that I am doing." From the start, the strongest and most bitter energies of the book were directed against the idea that art should serve a political cause, an idea that Auden had alternately embraced and rejected since 1932. When he gave a political speech in New York in March 1939, shortly before he began writing the book, he experienced his final revulsion against political action. As he told Mrs. Dodds in another letter: "I suddenly found I could really do it, that I could make a fighting demagogic speech and have the audience roaring. And, my dear, it is so exciting but so absolutely degrading; I felt just covered with dirt afterwards. It isn't that I think one shouldn't do any 'social' work but one must do something that is in one's nature to do, and for me that means 'teaching.' "

Auden took from Blake's *The Marriage of Heaven and Hell* the opposition between two basic human types, and his identification of the artist with the prolific and the politician with the devourer was his defiant refusal to interpret the artist as a servant to those who shape history or a parasite type on those who produce. "The Farmer—the Skilled Worker—the Scientist—the Cook—the Innkeeper—the Doctor—the Teacher—the Athlete—the Artist. Are there really any other occupations fit for human beings?" In contrast, the politicians, personified by "Judges, Policemen, Critics," are "the real Lower Orders, the low sly lives, whom no decent person should receive in his house."

Auden may first have noticed Blake's contrast between the two types early in the 1930s, when he read in Jung's *Psychological Types:* "Blake's intuition did not err when he described the two forms as the 'prolific' and the 'devouring.' " But Jung equated the prolific with the extravert, the devourer with the introvert, while Auden reversed the equation.

Auden spent much of the summer of 1939 on *The Prolific and the Devourer.* Recognizing that one of his models was Pascal, he began reading him by June and wrote a poem about him by August. Early that month he told Mrs. Dodds: "I've been hard at work at my pensées and so have had no time to write poetry."

Auden never finished the book and apparently abandoned it mid-September, when he lent some or all of the typescript to Selden Rodman. He told him it probably would not be published. In 1940 he incorporated some of the text into the "Notes" to "New Year Letter" that he published in his book *The Double Man* (1941). When he began work on *The Double Man* he still thought of the artist as one whom "The greatest of vocations chose." Around the time he finished *The Double Man* he returned to the Anglican Communion and recognized sainthood as the greatest of vocations. When Auden told Chester Kallman that he abandoned *The Prolific and the Devourer* because of its mandarin manner, he was evidently referring to its elevation of the artist's status and his own.

Auden had given up all hope in revolutionary politics when he worked on the book, but he retained his belief that inevitable historical processes would lead to a just society. That belief survived, with difficulty, the first weeks of the Second World War, but Auden abandoned it by the end of the year, when he began to turn from an optimistic humanism to a pessimistic Christianity.

In *The Prolific and the Devourer* Jesus is the greatest of historical thinkers, the first who understood the inevitable course of human society, the first who applied "the scientific approach to human behaviour—reasoning from the particular to the universal." Four years later, in Auden's essay "Purely Subjective" (*The Chimera*, Summer 1943), Jesus is the subject of a far more personal kind of understanding:

If a Christian is asked, "Why Jesus and not Socrates or Buddha or Confucius or Mahomet?" perhaps all he can say is: "None of the others arouse *all* sides of my being to cry 'Crucify Him.'"

Auden also rejected the pacifism of *The Prolific and the Devourer* in the early months of the war. He told Stephen Spender in 1941: "I have absolutely no patience with Pacifism as a political movement, as if one could do all the things in one's personal life that create wars and then pretend that to refuse to fight is a sacrifice and not a luxury."

The typescript of *The Prolific and the Devourer* is now in the Harry Ransom Humanities Research Center at the University of Texas at Austin, and it is reprinted here through the courtesy of the Center. Auden began by numbering the sections of the typescript but abandoned this scheme when he was almost finished with Part II. The last numbered section (115) is the section that begins "Epicurianism is only possible for the rich." Part I appeared in *Antæus* in 1976 and was reprinted in *The English Auden* in 1978. The full text first appeared in *Antæus* in 1981. Auden's chaotic typing is lightly corrected and emended in the text printed here, and two missing phrases have been restored between square brackets. The book, incidentally, has some minor lexicographical interest: its use of the word "a-political" predates by thirteen years the earliest use cited in the *Oxford English Dictionary*.

# PART I

*To the Devourer it seems as if the producer was in his chains: but it is not so, he only takes portions of existence and fancies in the whole.*

*But the Prolific would cease to be Prolific unless the Devourer, as a sea, received the excess of his delights.*

*These two classes of men are always upon earth, and they should be enemies: whoever tries to reconcile them seeks to destroy existence.*

—WILLIAM BLAKE
*The Marriage of Heaven and Hell*

No⊤ only does Man create the world in his own image, but the different types of man create different kinds of worlds. Cf. Blake: "A fool sees not the same tree that a wise man sees."

All the striving of life is a striving to transcend duality, and establish unity or freedom. The Will, the Unconscious, is this desire to be free. Our wants are our conception of what dualities exist, i.e., of what the obstacles are to our will. We are not free to will not to be free.

Freud has led us astray in opposing the Pleasure Principle to the Reality Principle. This is concealed Puritanism. "What I want, the world outside myself cannot give. Therefore what I want is wrong. The Death Wish: Never to have been born is beyond all comparison the best." On the contrary, my wants are just as much a part of reality as anything else.

It is untrue to say that we really desire to return to the womb. We picture freedom thus because it was our earliest experience of Unity and we can only picture the unknown future in terms of the known past.

At first the baby sees his limbs as belonging to the outside world. When he has learnt to control them, he accepts them as parts of himself. What we call the "I," in fact, is the area over which our will is immediately operative. Thus, if we have a toothache, we seem to be two people, the suffering "I" and the hostile outer world of the tooth. His penis never fully belongs to a man.

The Dictator who says "My People": the Writer who says "My Public."

People seem "real" to us, i.e., part of our life, in proportion as we are conscious that our respective wills affect each other.

Part of our knowledge of reality comes to us automatically through unavoidable personal contacts. The rest through the use of the intellect.

The intellect, by revealing to us unsuspected relations between facts of which we have no personal and therefore emotional experience and facts of which we have, enables us to feel about and therefore to be affected in our actions by the former. It widens the horizon of the heart.

The religious definitions of salvation (i.e., Unity or Freedom), "The Kingdom of Heaven," "In His Will is our

Peace," are the best because the most general. To be saved is to want only what one has.

To be wicked or neurotic in the moral or popular sense is to want what the majority do not want. To be wicked or neurotic in the religious or real sense is to want what one cannot have. These often coincide, but not always.

Even the ascetic who condemns all who consciously seek honour, power, and the love of women is less evil than the psychologist who condemns as neurotic all who don't. Judge not.

The neurotic is someone who draws a false general conclusion from a particular instance. X was once slapped unjustly by his papa and goes through life thinking that the world must always treat him unjustly. Sometimes the identification is only partial: symbolic fears—lobsters and castration.

There is only one salvation but there are as many roads thither as there are kinds of people.
  Three kinds of people: three roads to salvation.
  Those who seek it
    (1) through the manipulation of non-human things: the farmer, the engineer, the scientist
    (2) through the manipulation of other human beings: the politician, the teacher, the doctor
    (3) through the manipulation of their own phantasies: the artist, the saint

Everyone combines these three lives in varying proportions, e.g., when we are eating we are scientists, when we are in company we are politicians, when we are alone we are artists. Nevertheless, the proportions vary enough to make individuals inhabit such different worlds that they have great difficulty in understanding each other.

In its essence, Science is the exercise of the faculties to secure our physical existence in the material world. The baby seeking the breast is a scientist.

Art is the spiritual life, made possible by science.

Material happiness is created by science.

Spiritual happiness is created by art.

Politics creates nothing, but is a technique for their distribution.

The average man, the man-in-the-street, is the person who is passive towards experience: his knowledge is limited to what comes to him automatically through immediate personal experience. The scientist, artist, and politician proper are intellectuals, i.e., they seek to extend their experience beyond the immediately given.

We are all of us average men outside our particular fields. If we are not politicians we fail to understand politics that lie outside personal relations, if we are not artists we fail to understand art that does not reflect our own private phantasies, if we are not scientists we are bewildered by science that is not obviously based on common-sense experience.

"Work" is action forced on us by the will of another. "Unless you do this, I won't give you anything to eat. Unless you learn this irregular verb, I shall beat you." When I was at school, lessons were play to me. Work meant playing football.

The goal of everyone is how to live without working. To do this one must either have inherited or stolen money, or one must persuade society to pay one for doing what one likes, i.e., for playing.

The true aim of the politician (whether a politician proper, teacher, doctor, etc.) should be the creation of a society where no one has to work, where everyone is conscious, that is, of what they like doing, and nothing else has to be done. The politician who begins at the other end and tries to persuade men that it is their social duty to like doing what has to be done (or more usually what he thinks has to be done) is a tyrant.

How often one hears a young man with no talent say when asked what he intends to do, "I want to write." What he really means is, "I don't want to work." Politics and science can be play too, but art is the least dependent on the good-will of others and looks the easiest.

The Ivory Tower. Like the Point, this is really only a useful mathematical concept without actual existence, meaning complete isolation from all experience. The closest approximation in real life is schizophrenia.

The commonest ivory tower is that of the average man, the state of passivity towards experience.

We can justly accuse the poets of the nineties of ivory-towerism, not because they said they were non-political, but because the portion of life which they saw as poets was such a tiny fragment. Politics and science, indeed, they saw as average men of their social position, education, and income.

"To know a lot about something and a little about everything" is a rotten maxim. Rather, first discover what manner of person you are, and then learn to see everything through the lens of your gift. One destroys one's ivory tower only when one has learnt to see the whole universe as an artist, or as a scientist, or as a politician.

"The Child is Father to the Man." We do not become a different person as we grow up, but remain the same from infancy to old age. Maturity, however, knows who he is, and childhood does not. To mature means to become conscious of necessity, to know what one wants and to be prepared to pay the price for it. Failures either do not know what they want, or jib at the price.

The Parable of the Labourers in the Vineyard. Nature has her favourites whom she lets have everything at sale-price. There are others who get nothing except at famine prices. But they must pay them all the same.

The youngest of three brothers, I grew up in a middle-class professional family. My father was a doctor, my mother had a university degree. The study was full of books on medicine, archaeology, the classics. There was a rain-gauge on the lawn and a family dog. There were family prayers before breakfast, bicycle rides to collect fossils or rub church brasses, reading aloud in the evenings. We kept pretty much to ourselves. Mother was often ill.

In one way we were eccentric: we were Anglo-Catholics. On Sundays there were services with music, candles, and incense, and at Christmas a crèche was rigged up in the dining-room, lit by an electric-torch battery, round which we sang hymns.

There I learnt certain attitudes, call them prejudices if you like, which I shall never lose: that knowledge is something to seek for its own sake, an interest in medicine and disease, and theology, conviction (though I am unaware of ever having held any supernatural beliefs) that life is ruled by mysterious forces, a dislike of strangers and cheery gangs, and a contempt for businessmen and all who work for profits rather than a salary (my father was in municipal medicine, not private practice).

My father's library not only taught me to read, but dictated my choice of reading. It was not the library of a literary man nor of a narrow specialist, but a heterogeneous collection of books on many subjects, and including very few novels. In consequence my reading has always been wide and casual rather than scholarly, and in the main non-literary.

As a child I had no interest in poetry, but a passion for words, the longer the better, and appalled my aunts by talking like a professor of geology. Today words so affect me that a pornographic story, for example, excites me sexually more than a living person can do.

Besides words, I was interested almost exclusively in mines and their machinery. An interest in people did not begin till adolescence.

My interest and knowledge were such that I deceived not only myself but my parents into thinking that it was a genuine scientific interest and that I was gifted to become, what I said I was going to become, a mining engineer. A psychologist, noticing that I had no practical mechanical gift whatsoever, would have realised that the interest was a symbolic one. From the age of four to thirteen I had a series of passionate love-affairs with pictures of, to me, particularly attractive water-turbines, winding-engines, roller-crushers, etc., and I was never so emotionally happy as when I was underground.

The same psychologist would have also detected easily enough the complexes which were the cause of these affairs, but what was important for the future was not the neurotic cause but the fact that I should have chosen to express my conflicts in symbolic phantasy rather than in action or any other way. I cannot now look at anything without looking for its symbolic relation to something else.

I doubt if a person with both these passions, for the word and for the symbol, could become anything but a poet. At any rate, when at the age of sixteen a schoolfriend casually asked me one day if I wrote poetry, I, who had never written a line or even read one with pleasure, decided at that moment that poetry was my vocation, and though, when I look at my work, I am often filled with shame and disgust, I know that, however badly I may write, I should do anything else even worse, and that the only way in which I shall ever see anything clearly is through the word and the symbol.

My political education began at the age of seven when I was sent to a boarding school. Every English boy of the middle class spends five years as a member of a primitive tribe ruled by benevolent or malignant demons, and then another five years as a citizen of a totalitarian state.

For the first time I came into contact with adults outside the family circle and found them to be hairy monsters with terrifying voices and eccentric habits, completely irrational in their bouts of rage and good-humour, and, it seemed, with absolute power of life and death. Those who deep in the country at a safe distance from parents spend their lives teaching little boys, behave in a way which would get them locked up in ordinary society. When I read in a history book of King John gnawing the rush-mat in his rage, it did not surprise me in the least: that was just how the masters behaved.

So, despite all I have learnt since, my deepest feeling about politicians is that they are dangerous lunatics to be avoided when possible, and carefully humoured: people, above all, to whom one must never tell the truth.

In an English Public School there are no economic classes, but instead rigid class divisions based on seniority. The new boy starts as a member of the proletariat, menial and exploited, climbs by his third year into the respectable bourgeoisie, and by his fifth if he is politically reliable has become a responsible policeman or civil servant, honoured by the confidence of the Cabinet which may even sometimes ask his advice.

An admirable laboratory for the study of class-feeling and political ambition.

Such a state seems to be of the kind in which each individual has an equal chance to rise, and social reward depends solely upon merit. No doubt this is preferable to one in which social position is fixed, but it is certainly no Utopia.

I soon learnt to distinguish three kinds of citizens: the political, the a-political, and the anti-political.

The political is one whose values coincide with the State values. In a school, he is athletic, a good mixer, ambitious but not too ambitious, moral but not too moral. He climbs the social ladder rapidly, becomes a competent, unimaginative administrator of laws the rightness of which he does not question, is approved of and happy.

The a-political is one whose interests are not those of the State but do not clash with them, which usually means that they have nothing to do with people. Perhaps he is a photographer or a bird-watcher or a radio mechanic. As he is only anxious to be left alone, he performs his social duties well enough to keep out of trouble, and climbs slowly to a position of obscure security. He is the natural and sensible anarchist.

The anti-political is one whose interests and values clash with those of the State. He is not interested in athletics and shows it, his moral behavior is incorrect, he deliberately sabotages. There are however two sub-species of the anti-political: the one who, were the values of society more to his taste, would become a-political, and the one who in that case would become political. The latter is the true revolutionary: his anarchism is only a means to a political end. Whether he is a potential reformer or a potential tyrant depends on whether or no his personal ambition is combined with intellectual ability.

I also learnt by bitter experience to recognise yet another type, the ambitious anti-political who, ashamed of not being a social success, tries to disguise himself as a political. It is this type that becomes the police informer or the sadistic bureaucrat.

School life taught me that I was an anti-political. I wanted to be left alone, to write poetry, to choose my own friends and lead my own sex-life. The Enemy was and still is the politician, i.e., the person who wants to organise the lives of others and make them toe the line. I can recognise him instantly in any disguise, whether as a civil servant, a bishop, a schoolmaster, or a member of a political party, and I cannot meet him however casually without a feeling of fear and hatred and a longing to see him (or her, for the worst ones are women) publicly humiliated.

At first I thought I was a simple a-political anarchist forced into being an anti-political saboteur by a peculiar environment, but when I became a schoolteacher I discovered that I had more political ambition, that I enjoyed influencing others more than I had imagined.

When I left school, I became for a few years a rentier, which meant that through the power of an allowance from my parents, the State for me ceased to exist.

It is easy to criticise the rentier for being a parasite upon the labours of others, but no one who is honest would not change places with him if he could. A private income enables its fortunate possessor to be affectionate, tolerant, gay, to visit foreign countries and mix with all kinds of people, and such civilisation as we have is largely the creation of the rentier class. Many of its members are selfish and unpleasant, but if they do harm, it is usually only to themselves, and I think it probable that the percentage of unpleasant people is lower than in any other class.

The so-called ivory-tower artist is supposed to be typically a rentier. In actual fact the intelligent and sensitive rentier writer, owing to his greater freedom of movement and lack of economic pressure to produce hurried work, has a deeper and wider experience of life than his poorer colleague who is condemned to a fixed job.

I notice with alarm that those political systems which to a greater or lesser degree attempt to remove economic pressures and incentives, seem compelled to substitute for them social and governmental ones, to resemble in fact, and far too closely for my liking, an English public school. The politician will have succeeded only when and if he can create a society that preserves the freedom from social pressure of the rentier class while removing the economic injustice on which it rests.

I do not know if this is possible, but even if it is, I am doubtful if the politician can ever make it his aim, for to achieve it would be to destroy his profession, since social pressure is as much his medium as language is that of the poet.

At twenty-two, my allowance stopped, I ceased to be a rentier and became a master in a preparatory boarding school for the sons of the well-to-do. The primitive tribe ruled by demons which had terrified and fascinated the small boy, now appeared to the employee in a more prosaic light as a private business enterprise operating under a laissez-faire capitalism, a shop in which, as in all other kinds of shop, success depended upon our ability to be more attractive to customers than our competitors. For the first time in my life I became aware of the power of money, the technique of advertisement, and the gullibility of the public.

Politically a private school is an absolute dictatorship where the assistant staff play, as it were, Goering Roehm Goebbels Himmler to a headmaster Hitler. There are the same intrigues for favour, the same gossip campaigns, and from time to time the same purges. No one who is dependent upon the good-will of others (and even headmasters are dependent upon the good-will of the parents, just as a dictator has to cajole the masses) can avoid becoming a politician, and that involves not only many disingenuous compliances but a good deal of downright lying.

To be forced to be political is to be forced to lead a dual life. Perhaps this would not matter if one could consciously keep them apart and know which was the real one. But to succeed at anything, one must believe in it, at least for the time being, and only too often the false public life absorbs and destroys the genuine private life. Nearly all public men become booming old bores.

It is folly to imagine that one can live two lives, a public and a private one. No man can serve two masters.

In the struggle between the public life and the private life, the former will always win because it is the former that brings home the bacon.

To survive spiritually as a member of an organisation, one must possess some special talent which makes one so indispensable that almost any outrageous behavior is pardoned. Prostitutes and opera singers survive revolutions.

There is one other way. The anarchist hidden in the heart of everyone, even the administrator, has made every society tolerate and even demand the existence of The Fool, the licensed buffoon critic. Witness the popularity of Charlie Chaplin and the Marx Brothers. But it only tolerates a very few, and furthermore, this enviable position is precarious. At any moment the Fool may go too far and be whipped.

Teaching is a political activity, a playing at God the political father, an attempt to create others in one's own likeness. Since every individual is unique, this self-reproduction is luckily impossible. Bad teachers do not know this, or fondly imagine that they are not trying to interfere.

A teacher soon discovers that there are only a few pupils whom he can help, many for whom he can do nothing except teach a few examination tricks, and a few to whom he can do nothing but harm. The children who interested me were either the backward, i.e., those who had not yet discovered their real nature, the bright with similar interests to my own, or those who, like myself at their age, were school-hating anarchists. To these last I tried, while encouraging their rebellion, to teach a technique of camouflage, of how to avoid martyrdom. For the political I could do nothing except try to undermine their faith.

A teacher who keeps in touch with his pupils after they have left school and gone into the world is in a peculiarly advantageous position to study the effect on a person of his job.

Occupational diseases. A political problem of the first order. A large percentage of the occupations open to people today do them harm.

The Victorian father who said he would rather see his daughter dead than on the stage was less foolish than the modern parent who cheerfully allows his children to go into advertising or journalism.

His occupation dictates to a man what he does and selects his company. His actions and his company make the man. There is no such thing as an idealistic stockbroker.

One cannot walk through a mass-production factory and not feel that one is in Hell. And no amount of Workers' Control will alter that feeling.

There is a merciful mechanism in the human mind that prevents one from knowing how unhappy one is. One only realises it if the unhappiness passes, and then one wonders how on earth one was ever able to stand it. If the factory workers once got out of factory life for six months, there would be a revolution such as the world has never seen.

The Farmer—the Skilled Worker—the Scientist—the Cook—the Innkeeper—the Doctor—the Teacher—the Athlete—the Artist. Are there really any other occupations fit for human beings?

Judges, Policemen, Critics. These are the real Lower Orders, the low, sly lives, whom no decent person should receive in his house.

Lucky indeed the young man who is conscious of a vocation such as scientific research which is recognised and rewarded by society, and smooths his path to the Good Life.

Many careers are closed to me because I lack the necessary qualifications. I have no mathematical understanding; I can never become an engineer. But of those that remain open to me there are some which will employ my talents to make me more and more human, and others which, employing exactly the same talents, will make me more and more brutish. The Doctor and the Public Hangman require the same qualifications.

But, you will say, this is unrealistic bourgeois idealism. We must have policemen: only mass-production can bring motor-cars, refrigerators, electric razors within the pocket range of the workers. Perhaps you are right. Perhaps it is necessary that thousands should be martyred for the sake of that General Good which Blake called the plea of the hypocrite and the scoundrel. But neither I nor anyone I care for shall be among the martyrs if I can help it, and I find your complaisance disgusting.

Because the rich hypocritically denied the importance of material things, is no reason why Socialists should adopt the values of an American vacuum-cleaner salesman.

Distrust the man who says, "First things first! First let us raise the material standard of living among the Masses, and then we will see what we can do about the spiritual problems."

In accomplishing the first without considering the second, he will have created an enormous industrial machine that cannot be altered without economic dislocation and ruin.

Crisis. Civilisation is in danger. Artists of the world unite. Ivory Tower. Escapist. Ostrich.

Yes, the Crisis is serious enough, but we shall never master it if we rush blindly hither and thither in blind obedience to the frantic cries of panic.

Few of the artists who round about 1931 began to take up politics as an exciting new subject to write about, had the faintest idea what they were letting themselves in for. They have been carried along on a wave which is travelling too fast to let them think what they are doing or where they are going. But if they are neither to ruin themselves or harm the political causes in which they believe, they must stop and consider their position again. Their follies of the last eight years will provide them with plenty of food for thought.

If one reviews the political activity of the world's intellectuals during the past eight years, if one counts up all the letters to the papers which they have signed, all the platforms on which they have spoken, all the congresses which they have attended, one is compelled to admit that their combined effect, apart from the money they have helped to raise for humanitarian purposes (and one must not belittle the value of that) has been nil. As far as the course of political events is concerned they might just as well have done nothing. As regards their own work, a few have profited, but how few.

That movement will fail: the intellectuals are supporting it.

The World does not pardon political failure. No one can succeed at anything unless he is not only passionately interested in it, but absolutely confident of success. Are you so interested, are you so confident? If not, then you must be deaf to the voices of duty and your friend, the cries of the fatherless and of widows, for you cannot help them.

He who undertakes anything, thinking he is doing it out of a sense of duty, is deceiving himself and will ruin everything he touches.

You cannot give unless you also receive. What is it that you hope to receive from politics? excitement? experience? Be honest.

The artist qua artist is no reformer. Slums, war, disease are part of his material, and as such he loves them. The writers who, like Hemingway and Malraux, really profited as writers from the Spanish Civil War, and were perhaps really of some practical use as well, had the time of their lives there.

The voice of the Tempter: "Unless you take part in the class struggle, you cannot become a major writer."

The value of a framework of general ideas, e.g., Catholicism or Marxism, in organising the writer's experience, varies from writer to writer. One can point to Dante as a proof of their value, and to Shakespeare as a proof of their unimportance. But the value of such a framework lies, not in its scientific truth, but in its immediate convenience. A scientific hypothesis is a provisional framework for organising future experience: an artistic Weltanschauung is a fixed framework chosen by the artist as the most suitable for the organisation of past experience.

To be useful to an artist a general idea must be capable of including the most contradictory experiences, and of the most subtle variations and ironic interpretations. The politician also finds a general idea useful, but for his purpose, which is to secure unanimity in action, subtlety and irony are drawbacks. The political virtues of an idea are simplicity and infallibility.

"How can one think to fill people with blind faith in the correctness of a doctrine if by continued changes in its outward construction one spreads uncertainty and doubt?" (Hitler)

The artist's maxim: "Whoso generalises, is lost."
The politician's maxim: "Hard cases make bad law."

We do not criticise the artists of the past for holding religious or political or scientific beliefs which differ from our own. We do so criticise contemporary artists, because we are perplexed by our age and, looking round desperately for the answers to our problems, blame all indiscriminately who fail to give them, forgetting that the artist is not pretending to give an answer to anything.

Artists, even when they appear to hold religious or political dogmas, do not mean the same thing by them as the organisers of their church or party. There is more in common between my view of life and that of Claudel than there is between Claudel's and that of the Bishop of Boston.

The Prolific and the Devourer: the Artist and the Politician. Let them realise that they are enemies, i.e., that each has a vision of the world which must remain incomprehensible to the other. But let them also realise that they are both necessary and complementary, and further, that there are good and bad politicians, good and bad artists, and that the good must learn to recognise and to respect the good.

On meeting a stranger, the artist asks himself: "Do I like or dislike him?"

The politician asks: "Is he a Democrat or a Republican?"

Writers who try, like D. H. Lawrence in *The Plumed Serpent,* to construct political systems of their own, invariably make fools of themselves because they construct them in terms of their own experience, and treat the modern State as if it were a tiny parish and politics as if it were an affair of personal relations, whereas modern politics is almost exclusively concerned with relations that are impersonal.

Thus Lawrence's dictum "Anger is sometimes just, justice is never just," which is admirable advice to lovers, applied politically can only mean: "Beat up those who disagree with you."

One of the strongest appeals of Fascism lies in its pretence that the State is one Big Family: its insistence on Blood and Race is an attempt to hoodwink the man-in-the-street into thinking that political relations are personal. The man-in-the-street whose political education is confined to personal relations, and who is bewildered by and resentful of the impersonal complexity of modern industrial life, finds it hard to resist a movement which talks to him so comfortingly in personal terms. One of the best reasons I have for knowing that Fascism is bogus is that it is much too like the kinds of Utopias artists plan over café tables very late at night.

Works of art are created by individuals working alone. The relation between artist and public is one to which, in spite of every publisher's trick, laissez-faire economics really applies, for there is neither compulsion nor competition. In consequence artists, like peasant proprietors, are anarchists who hate the Government for whose interference they have no personal cause to see the necessity.

I have never yet met a Left-Wing intellectual for whom the real appeal of Communism did not lie in its romantic promise that with the triumph of Communism the State shall wither away.

Similarly, if one reads, say, the poems of Roy Campbell, it is not hard to see that to him Fascism means a heroic life of bull-fighting, motor-racing, mounting beautiful women, and striding bare-headed and square-shouldered magnificently towards the dawn.

The fate of Gide and Unamuno testify to what happens when the artistic dream is confronted with the political reality.

A desire for fresh experiences, humanitarian indignation at injustice and cruelty, are, even if short-sighted, at least honourable motives for taking to politics. But there are others, and few of us are quite innocent of them, which are less pretty.

In our political activities there is a larger element of old-fashioned social climbing than we care to admit. To receive social approval, to have one's work praised, even for the wrong reasons, is always gratifying, but it does not make for either artistic or political success. I have spoken too often myself about the need for popular art to feel comfortable when I hear this subject mentioned.

"Among the hardest workers in political parties will be found, like Rimbaud at Harrar, those whom the God has deserted." (Connolly)

Too often, alas, instead of cheerfully admitting the desertion, and betaking themselves to activities to which they are better fitted, they cannot leave the arts alone, but set up as critics. The bitterness of failure distorts everything they write.

There are many people, and they number some artists among them, who today seek in politics an escape from the unhappiness of their private lives, as once people sought refuge in the monastery and convent. Driven by envy and hatred they spread discomfort wherever they go and ruin everything they touch. A wise political party will have nothing to do with them.

But if artists are silly about politics, so are politicians about art. In the past it was sometimes possible for an individual of a secure ruling class to have the leisure to become a connoisseur as well as a politician. But not today.

Modern State patronage of the Arts. How awful it is. Think of the buildings in Washington. Think of those gigantic statues set up all over the world representing the Worker, the Triumph of Fascism, the Freedom of the Press. Think of the National Anthems.

Artists and politicians would get along better in a time of crisis like the present, if the latter would only realise that the political history of the world would have been the same if not a poem had been written, not a picture painted or a bar of music composed.

If the criterion of art were its power to incite to action, Goebbels would be one of the greatest artists of all time.

Tolstoy, who, knowing that art makes nothing happen, scrapped it, is more to be respected than the Marxist critic who finds ingenious reasons for admitting the great artists of the past to the State Pantheon.

# PART II

*For One is perfect and good being at unity in himself.*
*For Two is the most imperfect of all numbers.*
*For everything infinitely perfect is Three.*

—CHRISTOPHER SMART

NEVERTHELESS, whoever you are, artist, scientist, or politician, there remains the problem of how you are to live. Personal salvation, whatever you do or pretend, that is what you are really after, not the salvation of others. That you may occasionally be permitted to do, but only by the way. As a conscious goal, it is nothing but the conceit of the tyrant.

"We are all here on earth to help others: what on earth the others are here for, I don't know."

Let us start, like Pascal, with one observation and one assumption:

That, on the whole, Man is more often unhappy than happy.

That this unhappiness is unnatural: Man not only desires happiness but *ought* to be happy.

No one has ever seriously denied the observation, though some, like Pascal, have exaggerated the unhappiness. Men can only desire happiness because at moments they have experienced it or observed it in others.

The assumption has frequently been denied in part: i.e., as regards this temporal material world; to deny it in toto is to deny the rationality of the universe, though this too has been done.

If we accept both, then it follows:
1. (1) That there are laws which govern human life.
2. (2) That happiness is what we feel when we are living according to these laws, and unhappiness what we feel when we are not.
3. (3) That for the most part we do not live according to these laws.

But these laws, like the laws of Science, are not to be compared with human political laws. Human law is a generalised will imposed by force upon particular wills. If the law is broken it does not cease to be the law. In these laws, however, call them for convenience divine laws, there can be no opposition between the will of the whole and the separate wills of the parts. They are simply what happens if there is no interference from outside. Our knowledge of these laws is derived from our observation of particulars. If we can find one single exception, it means, not that the laws do not exist, but that our formulation of them is incorrect.

There are two and only two philosophies of life, the true and the false; all the apparently infinite varieties are varieties of the false. Or rather there is only the True Way and the false philosophies. For the Way cannot be codified as a philosophy: that would be to suppose that perfect knowledge of the whole of reality is possible, indeed that it is already known. The Way is only a way, the method we must adopt if we are to obtain any valid knowledge.

The false philosophy in all its forms starts out from a dualistic division between either the whole and its parts, or one part of the whole and another. One part is good with absolute right to exist unchanged; the other is evil with no right to exist. Progress consists in a struggle between the two in which the good is victorious, and salvation is only attained with the complete destruction of the evil. The dualism may be a supernatural and theological one, God and Satan, a metaphysical one, body and soul, energy and reason, or a political one, the philosopher king and the ignoble masses, the State and the individual, the proletariat and the masses.

Blake and the Marxists are probably correct in their diagnosis: Dualism is thinking about the creation in terms of man's experience of human politics. "King James was Bacon's Primum Mobile. . . . A tyrant is the worst disease and the cause of all others."

Human law rests upon Force and Belief, belief in its rightness. The Way rests upon Faith and Scepticism. Faith that the divine law exists, and that our knowledge of it can improve; and scepticism that our knowledge of these laws can ever be perfect: to have perfect knowledge we should have to know perfectly, i.e., become the universe.

Our grounds for Faith: the unhappiness of man.
Our grounds for Scepticism: the same.

We can only have belief in our personal sense experience of the present or past. I can believe that I saw a cow yesterday; I can only have faith [that I shall see a cow tomorrow]. But though Faith is not Belief, it is its effect. My faith that I shall see a cow tomorrow is conditional upon my belief that I saw a cow yesterday. Kafka is therefore wrong in saying: "Faith in progress does not mean faith that progress has already been made. That would be no faith." On the contrary, faith that progress will take place, on a basis of belief that no progress has so far been made, would not be faith but superstition. *Credo quia absurdum est.*

Let us begin then with what we know about the physical world:

(1) That existence is indestructible. Matter or energy can neither be created nor destroyed. All that can be changed are the forms in which it is organised.

(2) That existence is not static but in a constant state of change.

(3) That the physical world is apparently harmonious, and obeys regular laws, so that its behaviour is predictable.

(4) That Scientific Determinism does not, like Theological Predestination, presuppose a mysterious transcendent free-will operating upon a mass of inert particles. On the contrary every particle of matter has free-will, and what happens is simply the sum of the reactions of these free wills upon each other. Ability to predict what will happen, i.e., to see change as determined, is proportional

to the number of wills we can observe. It is impossible to predict the behaviour of a single atom in vacuo, but possible to predict the behaviour of a billion atoms in association.

Against Dualism, then, let us assert the following contraries:

(1) There are not "good" and "evil" existences. All existences are good, i.e., they are equally free and have an equal right to their existence. Everything that is is holy.

(2) No existence is without relation to and influence upon all other existences.

(3) Evil is not an existence but a state of disharmony between existences.

(4) Moral good is not an existence but an act, i.e., a rearrangement of existences which removes a disharmony.

(5) Our scientific knowledge is sufficient to justify our thinking that evil does not exist in the inorganic world. It is only with the appearance of life disharmony, i.e., absence of regularity, becomes observable.

(6) All living things, even the lowliest, show awareness of matter other than themselves, and their behaviour is in accordance with this awareness: "they take a portion of existence and fancy it the whole." Evil then is not a real disharmony in the nature of creation but local disturbances set up by the faulty behaviour of individual living

creatures, a behaviour caused not by a general corrupt will but their separate defective consciousnesses.

(7) "Active 'evil' is better than passive 'good.'"

It is not possible for an action to be evil in intention, for that would be to deny the right to exist of that part of the creation which is its agent, nor is it possible for it to be evil in its ultimate effects, for the effects of an act are infinite and that would mean that a single act could destroy all the previous regularities in the universe and it would be impossible to observe any regularities. An act is evil in so far as it is misdirected, so that it fails to achieve its intention directly, but instead achieves it by a roundabout series of mutually negating collisions and reactions. Misdirection of intention is possible because the agent is unaware or misinformed of the nature and extent of its relations with other agents, which is the same thing as saying that it is misinformed of its own nature.

Pure evil would be pure passivity, a denial by an existence of any relation with any other existence. This is not possible even to electrons.

(8) To do evil is to act contrary to self-interest. It is possible for all living creatures to do this because their knowledge of their self-interest is false or inadequate. Thus the animals whose evolution is finished, i.e., whose knowledge of their relations to the rest of creation is fixed, can do evil, but they cannot sin.

But we, being divided beings composed of a number of selves each with its false conception of its self-interest, sin in most that we do, for we rarely act in such a way that even the false self-interests of all our different selves are satisfied. The majority of our actions are in the interest of one of these selves, not always the same one, at the expense of the rest. The consciousness that we are acting contrary to the interests of the others is our consciousness of sin, for to sin is consciously to act contrary to self-interest. That our conception of this self-interest may be and indeed always is false, does not affect our consciousness of guilt. That is why when we look at men, we always find evidence of guilt, but the objects and actions about which guilt is felt vary so widely that the only generalisation we can make with certainty is of the universality of guilt, i.e., that conceptions of self-interest vary but are always false.

For if our different selves had true knowledge of their respective self-interests, it would be impossible for us to act except in a way that satisfied them all, for they would know that their interests are the same, and we should become, not only an undivided consciousness and so, like the animals, unable to sin, but also an undivided consciousness with a true knowledge of itself and so unable to do evil.

The Fall of Lucifer is a myth about the creation of life: The serpent cannot eat of the tree of the knowledge of good and evil himself: he can only tempt Eve to do so. He can do evil but he cannot sin, and so can go naked.

The Fall of Man does not mean that there was once a time when he did no evil, only that there was once a time when he did not sin. The Romantics, Rousseau, Lawrence, etc., would attempt to return to this state. This is a vain hope, but equally vain is the hope of the ascetic dualists like Pascal that man can attain a state where he can sin but not do evil.

The Fall is repeated in the life history of each individual, so that we have a double memory of Eden, one from personal experience, and one social-historical. These two memories are not always identical.

Forgiveness of sins does not mean that the effect of our acts is annulled, but that we are shown what that effect is. This knowledge, which is our only punishment, the punishment consisting in knowing that we have failed in our intention, removes our sense of guilt, for guilt is in part ignorance of the exact effect of our act upon others, and in part a dread that upon ourselves it has had no effect at all, that we are so unimportant as to be beneath the notice of the Divine justice.

Our conscience is our knowledge of the effect of our actions. It is not inborn in us—a baby has no conscience—but is the fruit of experience.

It is legitimate to speak of the Evil One, not because he exists. There is only our own state of fear and faithlessness, our mood of denial, but it is a mood we experience so often, and the experience in the most diverse situations is so identical, that it takes on for us all the attributes of a personality. Psychoanalysts call him the Censor.

We never meet very many, but each of us in the course of his life meets a few persons of whom he can only feel that they are damned, and more often than not they are intelligent sensitive people in good positions.

The gates of Hell are always standing wide open. The lost are perfectly free to leave whenever they like, but to do so would mean admitting that the gates were open, that is to say that there was another life outside. This they are afraid to admit, not because they get any pleasure from their present existence, but simply because the life outside would be different, and if they admitted its existence they would have to lead it. They know all this. They know that they could leave and they know why they don't. Their knowledge is the flame of Hell.

Many of the people we meet, perhaps the majority, are in the position of the good pagans in the Inferno. Without hope they live in desire. But Limbo is the lowest circle of Purgatory, not the uppermost circle of Hell. They do not deny, they are willing, but they have never been taught.

"What are beyond those hills? More hills."
    Paradise is a state of harmony of understanding. We are always entering paradise but only for a moment, for in the instant of achieving a harmony we become aware that the

whole which had previously seemed the limit of our consciousness is in its turn part of a larger whole and that there is a new disharmony to be reconciled.

This awareness that paradise must be continually lost, that if we try to remain in it Paradise will turn into Hell, is the pain of Purgatory, *La nostalgie des adieux.*

The memory of the bliss of Paradise is what gives us the courage to enter Purgatory again with hope to regain it. If we never experienced that happiness, we could not have faith.

The moral ideas of a society are its ideas of what it is necessary to do and to avoid doing in order to survive. What it thinks necessary will depend on many factors, environment, technological and political development, etc. Further there are certain actions which are in fact really necessary. Thus at any given moment there are divine laws for any given society as well as the human conception of them, however erroneous the latter may be.

As a society changes, the divine laws change too. General inertia and the advantages which its ruling class receive from the human laws make the development of the latter lag behind the former. Human laws which were once a reasonably approximate reflection of the divine laws cease to be so. When the strain which this discrepancy sets up reaches a certain point, it enters the consciousness of the more sensitive individuals as a feeling of guilt.

There are thus two competing sources of guilt: one arising from the breaking of the human law in the rightness of which one believes, as a dog feels guilty when he makes a mess in the house, and the other from a consciousness that the human law no longer corresponds to the divine, a conviction that unless the human law is broken society will perish.

It is only possible to want to break the human law because the individual members of a society are at different stages of development (e.g., children and adults) and are developing at different rates. The more complex, economically and politically, the life of society becomes, the fewer the individuals to whose will the human law fits exactly and the fewer will obey it naturally. Hence the more necessary it will become to enforce obedience either by direct coercion, the cultivation of fear, or by education, the cultivation of feelings of guilt.

As society becomes more and more complex, i.e., as the lives of individuals become more and more unique, the application of the divine laws becomes more and more a special application for each individual. It becomes, in fact, impossible to codify the divine laws. That is why the Catholic Church must always oppose "progress."

The Garden of Eden. The Golden Age. This does not mean that there was once a time when Man was good, only that there was once a time when society was simpler and more homogeneous, when it seemed possible to codify the divine laws; i.e., human law was not felt as coercive or imperfect. It was still possible to live by belief, and not yet necessary to live by faith.

Primitive religions are practical and political: a list of actions to do and actions to perform in order to survive from one day to the next. This do, and thou shalt live. The wages of sin is death. They assume that society will always remain the same.

Advanced religions are based on the knowledge that society is changing, and attempt to forecast the direction of change. They conceive of an ideal society in the future, try to deduce what its divine laws will be, and set them down now so that when man has reached that stage, he will be prepared and know how to act. Until then he must necessarily be sinful.

Our judgement of the great religions will depend upon our estimate of the accuracy of their historical forecast.

Jesus convinces me that he was right because what he taught has become consistently more and more the necessary and natural attitude for man as society has developed the way it has, i.e., he forecast our historical evolution correctly. If we reject the Gospels, then we must reject modern life. Industrialism is only workable if we accept Jesus' view of life, and conversely his view of life is more workable under industrialism than under any previous form of civilisation. Neither the heathen philosophers, nor Buddha, nor Confucius, nor Mohammed showed his historical insight.

Epicurianism is only possible for the rich, Stoicism for the highly educated. Buddhism makes social life impossible; Confucianism is only applicable to village life; Mohammedanism becomes corrupt in cities.

"By their fruits ye shall know them."

If there is one method in which we have faith today, and with reason, for it has consistently succeeded, it is the Scientific method of Faith and Scepticism. If there is one method which has consistently failed it has been the method of dogmatic belief backed by Force. But this criterion by observable results is in itself a scientific not a dogmatic criterion. For what is the Scientific attitude but the attitude of love, the love that does not reject even the humblest fact, the love that resists not evil (recalcitrant evidence) nor judges, but is patient, believing all things, hoping all things, enduring all things.

The teaching of Jesus is the first application of the scientific approach to human behaviour—reasoning from the particular to the universal. The Church only too rapidly retreated to the Greek method of starting with universals and making the particulars fit by force, but the seed once sown, grew in secret. What we call Science is the application of the Way to our relations with the non-human world.

Any religious teaching is, at bottom, prudent advice to the human race about how to be successful in the evolutionary struggle. This do, and thou shalt live. The wages of sin is death. Belief in a supernatural world after death only means belief in a continued evolution.

"If a man love not his brother whom he hath seen, how shall he love God whom he hath not seen?"

"What man is there of you, whom if his son ask bread will he give him a stone? Or if he ask a fish, will he give him a serpent?"

Both in the substance and the parabolic method of his teaching about love, Jesus never asks anyone to accept anything except on the basis of their personal experience of human love. In using the terms Father and Son to express the relation of the divine and the human, rather than, say King and subject, he makes the relation a physical not an intellectual one, for it is precisely because in the relation of parent and child the physical material relation is so impossible to deny, that it is so difficult for a human parent not to love their children irrespective of their moral judgement. They can do so, but it is very much more difficult for them than for those who have not such an obvious physical connection. Jesus in fact is asserting what the psychologists have confirmed: that one does in fact always conceive of one's relations with life in terms of one's relations with one's parents, and in proportion as these were bad, one's attitude to life is distorted. But though parental love is often imperfect, it is good enough and often enough for us to have no doubt about what it should be like. We expect parents to love their children whether they act well or badly because it is our experience that they usually do: we expect a physical relation to override morals. In speaking of the fatherhood of God, Jesus is teaching that God does not love us because we are "good" or because he is very "good" and merciful but because he has to, because we are part of him, and he can no more hate us if we act badly than a man can hate one of its fingers when it aches: he can only want it to get well.

"Thou shalt love thy neighbour as thyself."

Again Jesus bases love on the most primitive instinct of all, self-preservation. Those who hate themselves will hate their neighbours or endow them with romantic perfections. The Neo-Romantics like Nietzsche and D. H. Lawrence have misread this text as "Thou shalt love thy neighbour MORE than thyself," and base their attack upon Christianity upon this misreading, plus a lot of false biology about cave-man nature and the struggle for existence. Jesus never said this, only the churches.

On the contrary, at the last supper, he took eating, the most elementary and solitary act of all, the primary act of self-love, the only thing that not only man but all living creatures must do irrespective of species, sex, race, or belief, and made it the symbol of universal love.

"Suffer little children to come unto me for of such is the Kingdom of Heaven."

Time and again Jesus attacks those who think of the good life as something contrary to our animal nature, that the flesh is not divine. The philosophers had all said: "You do not of course want to love your neighbour but you must because it is your duty and you will be punished if you don't."

>Look upward, working out the beast
>And let the ape and tiger die.

Jesus on the other hand says: "You can love your neighbour, not because you ought to, but because you really want to, because that is the nature of the particular biological species to which you belong. You are neither an ape nor a tiger by nature, and if you want proof of this, if you want to know what your biological nature is like, look at your children, whom you must admit do love and trust their neighbour naturally unless their trust is betrayed, and quite irrespective of their sex or class or colour or morality, to your great embarrassment."

The biologists have confirmed Jesus both as to our biological descent and as to the relation of love and intelligence. They have shown that the stock from which man springs was non-aggressive, affectionate and social, with a communal life based on a larger social unit than the family, and a long period of immaturity needing parental care.

In the study of intelligent behaviour in animals they have also found that intelligence only functions when the animal is unafraid. An atmosphere of love and confidence is essential.

If the problem set is too difficult or the investigator is impatient the reaction of fear sets in and paralyses the intelligence. In other words love biologically precedes intelligence. Man is the most intelligent animal precisely because he is the most affectionate.

For the tiger, maybe, whoso saveth his life, saveth it, but not for man.

Hence the practical advice of Jesus on how to succeed in this life: "Seek ye first the kingdom of heaven and all these things shall be added unto you." For lack of faith, hatred, are lethal to intelligence, and so, for an intelligent animal, to survival.

"The Kingdom of Heaven is within you."

"The Kingdom of Heaven is like unto a grain of mustard seed, etc."

"Except a grain of wheat fall into the earth and die, it abideth alone, but if it die, it bringeth forth much fruit."

"Except a man be born again, etc."

In attacking dualist doctrines of the Higher and Lower self, and placing the source of our love in our animal childish nature, Jesus does not fall into the Romantic error of denying the necessity for growth, or saying that it is wrong to grow up and that man has no future. On the contrary he uses man's known past as the basis for faith in his unknown future. If our animal nature did not offer us proofs of the Way, we could have no faith, we could only have superstition and blindly obey some authority. All the metaphors that Jesus uses to describe spiritual growth are biological metaphors, i.e., he asserts that growth is continuous. For the seed does not in fact die, but is changed into something else. Even an abrupt mutation is only a re-organisation of elements already existing. We are not asked to destroy or deny any part of our nature but to allow it to grow and be converted. Pascal and Rousseau both lacked faith and made growth impossible, one by depriving man of the necessary energy, the other by depriving him of the necessary intelligence.

The difference between the child and the mature man is firstly an increase in faith based on experience, and secondly an increase in conscience based on knowledge of the effects of his acts. He is able to love those who have injured him, while the child cannot do this; he is able to understand the intention behind the act. He no longer wants to make mistakes in conduct that the child makes by necessity because it can only see the immediate effect.

"He is not the God of the dead, but of the living."

Jesus took such care to avoid making any statement for or against survival after death and the existence of a supernatural world that one can only conclude that he considered this belief unimportant, but anxiety about it dangerous.

There may or may not be a supernatural world, but to think like Pascal that its existence or non-existence should make any difference to our life here, is to suppose a suspension in the chain of causality, or rather a division into two streams, one operating normally in this world, and the other mysteriously arrested, to begin operating mysteriously after death.

It is as if there were two Gods, the Mammon of Unrighteousness ruling the natural world, and the God of Righteousness ruling the next. You cannot avoid breaking the laws of one, but as the former can only punish you for seventy years and the latter can punish you for ever, the prudent man will put his money on the second and disobey the first.

This is the sin against the Holy Ghost, which is to deny the Unity of Truth. It is pardonable to sin against the Father, i.e., to think that life is ruled by fear and not by love, and it is pardonable to sin against the Son, i.e., to hate men who have injured one, because these sins are due to ignorance and natural fear. But to believe in two sets of truth is to believe what one's reason knows to be false.

Those who bother about life after death are either the victims of worldly injustice which they have been tricked into accepting as just, or the damned who hope against hope that damnation is not eternal. For the Divine Law, whatever its nature, operates here and now. As Kafka says: "Only our concept of Time makes it possible for us to speak of the Day of Judgement by that name; in reality it is a summary court in perpetual session."

I feel about Pascal as Pascal felt about Montaigne. Of all the dualists he is incomparably the noblest and most seductive. Like most of us he exalted the faculty he lacked over the faculty he possessed, the heart over the reason, and fashioned an image out of his opposite. The neurotic who as a child was thrown into fits by the sight of his two parents together was truly a split being with a corrupt heart and an uncorrupt intelligence.

By all appearances he should have been damned, but he was saved, and saved not as he thought by his heart but by his reason, for it was his reason that told him that his heart was corrupt and that therefore the love of human beings was not for him.

"In these three questions (the three temptations in the wilderness) the whole subsequent history of mankind is, as it were, brought together into one whole, and foretold, as in them are united all the unsolved historical contradictions of human nature."—Dostoyevsky

*Command that these stones be turned into bread.*

The conversion of stones into bread would be a supernatural miracle. It would mean that there were two sets of laws, the scientific laws of this world and the superior divine laws of a supernatural world.

There is only one way in which stones can be turned into bread, and that is by phantasy, stimulated by hunger. In our popular literature where the scullery maid marries the Prince Charming this and similar miracles are being constantly performed.

Primitive peoples and children begin by thinking that their will is omnipotent. A thing is what I want it to be. *"L'état c'est moi."* They begin with belief, belief in themselves.

They have to be weaned slowly and carefully from this belief for if it is shattered too suddenly, they switch over abruptly from belief in their omnipotence to belief in their absolute impotence: they suffer a psychological trauma and their growth is arrested. For growth consists in the abandonment of belief and the acquisition of faith, and they have only passed from one belief to another.

Satan knows that the miracle is impossible, and hopes by persuading Jesus to attempt it, to destroy his faith in the shock of failure.

*If thou be the Son of God, cast thyself down.*

Again an attempt to destroy faith by urging the performance of an impossible miracle. The first temptation was the temptation of childhood, this of adolescence.

The child believes in the omnipotence of his sensual desires. As he grows he discovers that this is not so, and becomes conscious of himself as an I separated sharply from the rest of the universe, and further a thinking I, a consciousness to which his physical self is as much an object of thought as are other people and things. For the child's belief in the omnipotence of animal desire, he exchanges a belief in the omnipotence of the intellect: instead of thought being a creation of desire (the phantasy of the universe as bread), matter is a creation of thought. I can throw myself down from the temple because the temple, the street, gravity only exist if I choose to think they do. I can think them away.

Jesus might well have answered the second temptation by reversing his answer to the first: "Man does not live by words alone but by the bread that proceedeth daily from the hand of God. I and my Father are one."

*All these will I give thee if thou wilt fall down and worship me.*

The first two temptations were concerned with miracles, with belief in the absolute freedom of the will, conceived either as desire or as thought. The last temptation, the temptation of maturity, is concerned, not with Belief but with Faith. Unable to tempt Jesus into false beliefs, Satan appeals to reason.

"Of course," he says, "I never imagined that you would fall for the childish tricks I tried to play on you. You are a grown-up person with a wide experience of the world. And I realise now that you and I are colleagues, who share a common passion for the truth. Like myself you are a person of faith: we both believe that the divine law exists and that it is possible to discover something about it, though we both know that all dogmas and doctrines are at best provisional makeshifts which as time goes on become outmoded and misleading.

"I always tell men, and I expect you do too, not to trust to beliefs and authorities but to search their own experience. 'The Kingdom of Heaven is within you,' I tell them, 'Ask and ye shall receive. Seek and ye shall find.' For there is only one test of the accuracy of our knowledge of the truth, and that is our experience of success or failure. The true Way is the way which works.

"Forgive me if I am boring you with what you know already, but they tell me that you are going round teaching men that the True Way is to love the truth with all their hearts and to love their neighbours as themselves.

"I'm sure they must have muddled the second part of what you said—men never listen properly—for it seems to me to contradict the first. I cannot see how anyone who loves the truth can come to any conclusion but my own, namely, that the True Way is to see that one is stronger than one's neighbour, for the truth is that we love no one but ourselves and hate those who cross our will. That is the divine law and neither you nor I can alter it even if we wanted to, which we don't because we ourselves are subject to that law.

"So if you really did say what I was told you said, I implore you to look again at the world, at human history, in your own heart, and give yourself an honest answer, lest you fall into damnation, for what is damnation but to deny the truth when one has seen it."

In claiming to be able to offer Jesus the Kingdoms of this world, Satan is claiming to be God, for if the Kingdoms of this world are really his, then Jesus is mistaken.

The evidence on which Satan bases his argument may be found in many books, *The Republic, The Prince, Leviathan, Mein Kampf,* but nowhere perhaps more completely and cogently expressed than by the Grand Inquisitor in Dostoyevsky's *The Brothers Karamazov.* Jesus does not answer him, any more than he answered Satan or Pilate, because he does not need to: their own experience answers for them and they know very well what they do, and that they have failed, so that, tormented by the knowledge of failure and of the hate they have aroused, they cry:

"Why dost thou come to hinder us? And why dost thou look silently and searchingly at me with thy mild eyes? Be angry. I don't want your love."

But had he been listening, not to the Inquisitor himself, but to some attendant who was only repeating his master's words, he might have answered along some such lines as this, taking up the Inquisitor's main arguments in turn.

"Nothing has ever been more insupportable to man and a human society than freedom."

Your Master has told you that I offer Man freedom. I do, but that freedom is not a state of being equally free to do anything, of nothing seeming more necessary to do than another. That would be a state of loneliness and horror which would indeed be insupportable.

On the contrary I offer you the same freedom that he professes to offer you, the only freedom there is, the freedom to know the truth, which, when you once know it, you must either obey or perish.

The difference between us is that, while he professes to tell you what that truth is, I know that I cannot tell you. I can only tell you how to look for it. The truth is within you. Seek and ye shall find: knock and it shall be opened unto you.

I have my own experience of the truth, and I can try to express it in words if you like, but if my words mean anything to you, it is only because you recognise them as expressing knowledge which you already possessed. No one can come to me except the Father draw him. If you do not respond, then my picture of the truth is of no use to you, for though the truth is one, our vision of it and its application is unique for every nature, for we are created unique growing individual beings, two individuals can never become one, and there is no other way to the truth but through individual faith and individual effort.

All this your Master knows, but for the sake of that Libido Dominendi which he himself admits to be the deadliest of all the sins, he will not admit it to you.

He tells you that you are weak and sinful. You do not

need him to tell you that: your hourly experience tells you. But in claiming to be your infallible guide, he is claiming to be exempt from error. Do not be deceived by his false humility when he says: "I am a weak sinful individual like yourself, but the church and its doctrines of which I am a representative are infallible and necessary to salvation," for he knows very well that the church and the doctrines are human creations and subject to the same limitations as all others.

He tells you to rely on authority: this too you do not need to be told. In every activity and phase of your life you trust those who seem to have more experience than yourself, parents, teachers, friends, but only so far as what they say is confirmed or at least not contradicted by your own experience, when that happens you consult another or trust to yourself, for no authority is an authority which is not accepted voluntarily. This too your Master knows and for that reason must do his utmost to prevent your consulting any authority but himself: he must try to censor your reading and your company.

Certainly false prophets will come who will lead you astray if you let them. But no search for the truth is possible without mistakes. Without false prophets, there can be no true ones.

"The craving for community of worship is the chief misery of everyone individually and of all humanity since time began."

Again your Master has deceived you by a confusion of language. Worship is not any specific act or form of words or belief, but a state of love. Community of worship is any gathering of individuals in mutual love, where two or three are gathered in the name of love and truth. Such gatherings are taking place everywhere all the time, in a thousand different forms: in the meetings of lovers, family reunions, games, scientific or artistic discussions, gangs of workmen engaged on some piece of construction. Identity of belief is sometimes the cause of such a gathering but a rare one, and such gatherings must of necessity be small, for complete identity of belief between two persons is impossible and even approximate identity does not stretch very far.

Men do not crave identity of belief, they crave to give and to receive love. Your Master tries to persuade you that love is dependent upon identity of belief, that we can only love those who share our beliefs, but this is a lie, which your own experience of social intercourse disproves. People love each other primarily because they are fellow creatures of the same physical species and cannot get on without each other. That is why I chose as a type of community of worship the only act into which belief cannot enter, the only act in which universal community of worship is possible, because it is the common and primary interest of life, the satisfaction of physical hunger. It is your Master who makes a mystery of the last supper, not I. I tell you that even a Rotary Club dinner is nearer my intention than the Mass.

"We have corrected thy work and founded it on miracle, mystery, and authority."
Miracles are not, as your Master has taught you to think, supernatural interferences with natural laws, for the

Truth cannot be divided against itself. When your knowledge of some portion of creation reaches the point where you can see the causal relation between events accurately enough to predict the future, you call it a scientific or natural law. What you call miracles are events which occur contrary to your prediction, usually events which you would like to happen, for you do not commonly speak of an evil miracle. Your prediction was false because your knowledge was imperfect.

Everything that happens is a witness to the truth: the special value of miracles is that they reveal the imperfection of man's knowledge, and stimulate him to search further: they induce humility and curiosity. A miracle has not borne its full fruit until it is understood, that is, until it has ceased to be a miracle and can be repeated at will.

When I was on earth, I did many of these miracles: I healed the sick and cast out devils: but it was not I who did them, but the sick and possessed themselves, or rather the truth within them. All I did was to draw their attention to it, which I could only do on condition that they had faith, not in me, that what I told them was true. When I said to the sick of the palsy, "Thy sins are forgiven thee," I simply drew his attention to the true cause of his malady. It was not I who forgave him, nor even God. For it is not God who judges but Man. To be forgiven means to realise that one has never been judged except by oneself.

I was reluctant to have these miracles talked about because I knew very well the danger that men would make me personally responsible for them, and instead of thinking of me as a man with a clearer perception of truth than themselves, think of me as a special being exempt from the laws which governed their lives. This attitude is the sin of idolatry, for an idol is someone or something that one believes to be above the law, and to worship one, whether a person, or institution or dogma, is to abandon Faith for belief, Science for magic.

Nobody desires miracles more than your Master for he knows their usefulness in securing your belief in him, but in his very efforts to destroy your faith, he is taking away the one condition that makes them possible. But it is not possible to destroy faith entirely and miracles are always reoccurring, most of them outside his flock.

I was always being asked by whose authority I spoke and acted, and I always turned the question aside, because everyone knows the answer: that there is only one authority which it is impossible to disobey, our conception of the truth, whether that conception be correct or false. All other authority rests on force and is therefore unreal.

Over and over again I told my disciples that it was not I, Jesus, the son of a carpenter, living in Palestine during the Roman Empire, who was important, but the truth of which I was for the moment the mouthpiece. Over and over again I told them: "Call me not good. There is none good but God alone. You shall do greater miracles than I." In calling myself the Son of Man, I hoped to prevent them associating the truth with my personal existence. It was inevitable sooner or later that someone should be born who should discover the True Way. If it had not been me, then it would have been another. The great painters understood this, which is why they represented me either as an infant or as dead, i.e., as Man, not a man.

But my disciples and still more those who came after did not. Judas understood and in his disappointment betrayed me to the chief priests: but the others in their misunderstanding betrayed mankind. Your Master has founded the greatest organisation the world has ever seen upon me as a historical person. To believe in me and the historical accuracy of the legends which gathered round my name, to believe in the eternal truth of the intellectual constructions which learned men put upon my most casual remarks, has been made the only way of escape from persecution in this world and damnation in the next. Ignoring my prayer, man has been taught to believe in me, and to lose faith in him that sent me.

Small wonder then that when men, appalled at the corruption and tyranny and lying of the Church, rebel against it, my words and the false idol into which I have been made are so inextricably associated in their minds, that in rejecting the idol they also reject the words.

But Heaven and Earth shall pass away, but my words shall not pass away, for they are true, and therefore all that men do must confirm them. They have only to examine their successes and their failures, their own lives and history, to come to the same conclusions as I did, so that in a sense, it would not matter if I had never been born, indeed my words have been so betrayed and exploited that it may well be that men will have to forget all about me and rediscover the truth for themselves.

Nevertheless it will be a tragedy if this has to be, because millions of mankind will fail and suffer whose failure and suffering could be avoided, if only they will forget their resentment against those who claim to speak in my name, and will read my words as if they had never heard of me before.

I am content to abide by their judgement for there are not separate worlds of business, science, art, religion, with different laws: there is only life and truth, and if any words of mine were to be contradicted by human experience, they would be false, no matter who I claimed to be.

# PART III

*It is the world's one crime its young grow old,*
*Its poor are oxen, dull and leaden-eyed;*
*Not that they starve but starve so dreamlessly,*
*Not that they sow but that they seldom reap,*
*Not that they serve but have no Gods to serve,*
*Not that they die but that they die like sheep.*

—VACHEL LINDSAY

Progress is simply progress, i.e., going on and on in one direction. Whatever happens considered as a historical succession of events in which we can see a consistency of direction is progress. If what happens conflicts with our ideas of what ought to happen, this only means that our ideas of what ought to happen, our conception of progress, is false. A historical event is "good" or "bad" in the degree to which it furthers or hinders the succession of events in time which is history from moving in the general direction in which they are moving: i.e., in the degree to which it is in conformity with the divine law.

If Jesus was right, then:

    (A) The general direction of history must have been and be towards

        (1) The unity of mankind and a recognition of the common humanity of all men

        (2) The equality of men, through a recognition that all men are subject to the same divine law, and

(B)

      (1) The Way of love and understanding, which must by its very nature intend this direction, must always have assisted events so to move,

      (2) The Way of hate and coercion, whether it intended Unity and Equality or their opposites, must have always hindered events from so moving, but also must have always failed finally to prevent them.

If history does not offer this evidence, then Jesus was wrong, and Satan and the Inquisitor were right.

The unequivocally apocalyptic nature of the teaching of Jesus has at once been Satan's greatest hope of proving him wrong, and his greatest dread lest History should prove to mankind beyond a shadow of doubt that he was right.

Marxism has made an immense contribution to our understanding of history, in its emphasis on Man the Maker, the producer of wealth, as opposed to the obsession of earlier historians with Man the Politician, the consumer. It has made us realise that history is made up of an immense number of individual acts of which by far the greater number are not acts of warfare or diplomacy, but acts of physical work with physical materials, earth, stone, metal, etc., and that it is Man the Maker who is the prime cause of historical change, for he creates the wealth for the consumption of which Man the Politician struggles.

This is an antidote to the pessimism which the study of political history from Thucydides and Tacitus onwards must always induce. Politicians have always had a low opinion of human nature. But if their experience were all, if human action was all like the behavior of the Athenians at the Melian Conference, not only would the Gospels be wicked nonsense, but the human race would long ago have become extinct, for there would have been no wealth to fight for.

Man the Maker, i.e., man in his relation to the non-human world, as cultivator, herdsman, engineer, artist, has always followed the way of love. He discovered very early that it is useless to make moral judgements about Nature or to punish or even to try to coerce her, that practical success depended upon a harmonisation of his will with hers.

It is hard for a rich man to enter into the Kingdom of Heaven, not because wealth or even its possession is evil—wealth is always a good—but because the typical rich man is only a consumer, not a producer and consumer like the poor. His knowledge of human nature is therefore confined to his knowledge of Man the Politician, i.e., man in his relations with other men, to that sphere of human action where the Way of love is least practised. He is not totally without knowledge of the Way, for he like all men had parents, but it is harder for him to have faith than it is for the poor, who share his knowledge of Man the politician, but know Man the Maker as well, and so have a double-experience of the Way, one from their childhood and one from their adult practical life.

In its emphasis on the economic motives for human action, Marxism reveals not the selfishness of man, but the real basis of human love, which is not blood-kinship nor moral goodness or badness, but mutual need. We can love our neighbour as ourself because our need of each other is equal. There is no love without reciprocity, not even mother-love, for if the act of suckling did not satisfy sensual needs of the mother, the baby would die of starvation.

Only our corruption prevents us from realising that money is, in essence, only a technique for the extension of love in space and time.

Imperialism, i.e., all forms of exploitation, is possible for a time only because the exploited need the exploiters, that is to say, there is a real basis for love between them. It is unworkable in the long run because it fails to satisfy the needs, not of the exploited but of the exploiters.

For example, Imperialism begins by thinking it is possible to get rich by stealing, but ends by discovering that successful stealing ruins the thief. If it concentrates on home production then it finds itself faced with high wages at home and a foreign market too poor to buy. If it concentrates on foreign production with low labour costs it is faced with unemployment and poverty at home.

In saying "I want but don't need to be wanted, I love but don't need to be loved," Imperialism violates the laws of economics, which boil down to this: "It is impossible to receive without giving."

Though all our ideas true or false are the product of our experience, i.e., of our way of living, it is legitimate to see ideas as the prime agents of human historical change, for were it not for his capacity to think, man's evolution would be complete like that of the animals. An idea has two purposes, to justify our satisfactions, and to find a way to remove our wants. In its aspect as justification, an idea is a pure reflection of our material life and neither can re-enter history as an effective agent nor wants to. In its aspect as a means to remove wants, it demands a change in our actions and so becomes an agent of change. In so far as it is true, i.e., it achieves its conscious intention, the causal relation between idea and historical change is obvious—e.g., the historical effects of technical discoveries.

But in so far as it is false, though it is just as much an agent as if it were true, the effects which it produces are so different from its conscious intention, that we fail to see the causal relation between it and history, and see only its justificatory purpose, the more so because the principal obstacle to truth in our thinking is our desire for justification, so that the falser an idea the more obvious its justificatory element.

It is the different errors in all religious and political ideologies that have led men to the mistaken conclusion that such ideas are nothing but blindly determined reflections and in no sense free-willing agents.

Imperial Rome attempted to unify mankind and to establish the equality of all men before the human law. But by attempting to do this by force, and by making the human law unequal, i.e., by believing in Imperialism, she destroyed herself, and the result of her failure was the abandonment for centuries of faith not in her means, but her intention which was the establishment of the Good Life upon earth, and in their despair men fixed all their hopes upon personal immortality and the supernatural world.

For a few years after the crucifixion the Christians were sustained by the belief that the Parousia was coming within their lifetime and were able to practise the Way in their own lives, but their thinking was already dualistic: they had already lost faith in the Kingdom of Heaven within them: the Parousia was to be an outside interference occurring not as a result of their own efforts or those of future generations, but by an authoritarian act of the Divine Will. As soon as this hope faded, the consequences of their error became obvious. Unity and Equality were not possible in this world, except as unity and equality in Belief.

This perversion of the teaching of Jesus was not due to the conspiracy of a few theologians: it was the result of mass fear inspired by the collapse of the Roman attempt to build the City of God on earth.

Only those with sensory defects like the blind need belief in the nature of the physical world: our senses give normal men a common faith. But faith in a spiritual world of which we have no direct common experience can only be maintained if there is a unity of belief. If the existence of the spiritual world was the only guarantee that it was worth having been born, then infallible dogmas were indispensable to human life.

Its official adoption by Constantine was not the cause of the corruption of the Church. The world was demanding a universal supernatural religion, and the politicians were bound to adopt one or another. The Church did not become political and Mammon-worshipping because it was adopted by Caesar: it was adopted by Caesar because it was influential and rich.

Its paganisation was due to its misunderstanding of its own success, for it had succeeded not because of but in spite of its dualism, because it was less purely dualistic than its rivals, since whatever it might do, it was committed to teaching the way of love, and so was able to produce in those who followed it fruits of joy and peace which no rival could grow.

The Church was not wrong to be political—it could be nothing else. But if it had realised that its superiority lay not in its dogmas (though even these were superior) but in the Way which it taught, it would have used its political influence into furthering the Way and only incidentally into furthering the dogmas. By reversing the order of importance of these two, it was led inevitably to persecute. For granting the premise that the Way is an effect of belief, not a cause, the argument of the Inquisition is perfectly sound. The heretic is the worst of criminals because he threatens to make the Way impossible: it is more merciful to burn him now than to let him and those whom he might deceive suffer eternally.

In enlisting, not the Temporal power as such, but the temporal power in the form of the sword, the Church denied the source of its success and destroyed not The Way, but what it intended, Catholic Unity.

The Reformation was not a struggle between the Church and a rival heathen faith. Since the death of Jesus, there has never been a conflict between another faith and Christianity, in however backward bastardised a form, in which the latter has not been easily the victor: there has only been serious conflict between rival interpretations of the teaching of the Gospels.

As long as the rest of the world despaired of the future of the world even more than the Church, the Church with all its faults was the guardian and developer of civilisation, of Science, art, learning, etc. It was only as men recovered their nerve that the necessity for change became obvious.

The world was saved during the Middle Ages, as perhaps it always is, by the poor. It is impossible to lose faith in this world completely, for could this happen, men would neither till the soil nor beget children. Men went on living, trade expanded, and confidence in individual judgement. The Reformation was a class struggle of the poor and trading classes against the feudal nobility, but this does not mean that the exploiters were absolutely unjust and the exploited absolutely just, only that the latter as the producers of wealth can never lose faith in this world, and are compelled to approach correctly the study of the divine law which they have not seen, i.e., through the study of their neighbour whom they have seen. Trade always weakens dogmatic belief because it makes men realise that people with different beliefs have common needs, and that people with beliefs which one has been taught are wicked may be leading a life which one has been taught is good, i.e., that the connection between the Way and Belief is not absolute.

Caesarism had said in effect: Unity and Equality before the law are possible in this world, but can be achieved only by the sword. Catholicism said in effect: Unity is possible in this world, but not Equality. The two combined can only be realised in the next world, and not by following the way of the sword but by following the way of love. This world however is ruled by the sword, and you must keep yourself unspotted from the world if you can: for to follow the True Way means failure and poverty on earth.

But as a matter of fact you will not be able to keep yourself unspotted from the world because you have to live and eat: all men are sinners and it is impossible to follow the Way consistently.

The Church will overcome this dilemma for you. If you believe its dogmas, partake of its sacraments, and perform works of mercy, your sins shall be forgiven you and you shall be saved.

This dualism encouraged the Church to become worldly in a corrupt way for sensible men do not deliberately court failure in this world, particularly if they can square the next by apologies and ritual actions.

The reaction from this was to place Equality before Unity. Protestantism said in effect:

We agree that Unity and Equality are only to be found together in the next world and that this world is ruled by fear, but it is Equality that is possible in this world, not Unity. It is hypocrisy for the Catholics to tell you to keep yourselves unspotted from the world when as they admit it is impossible, and hypocrisy to say that poverty is good when their own conduct gives them the lie.

There are two Gods, the God of common-sense experience, the engineer who moves the stars and ordains the laws of economics and politics who knows nothing of love, and the God of love who can only be known by the private conscience.

It is sinful to disobey either, but [it is] impossible to avoid [doing so], but it is wicked pride on the part of the Catholics to pretend that a few ritual acts and works of charity will cancel our offences. Man is hopelessly wicked and helpless: he can only be saved because God chooses to save him, not for anything a man has done, but simply because God wills it.

In realising that the laws of this world are divine laws that must be understood and obeyed, Protestantism made science and material progress possible, but in thinking that these laws were incompatible with love, that the Way could only be practised as a private individual, not as a citizen, it achieved the opposite of what it intended. Just as Catholicism, which intended Unity and denied Equality, destroyed material Unity but preserved a certain spiritual Equality, so Protestantism, which intended Equality and denied Unity, destroyed spiritual Equality but created material Unity.

Science has made the world a single economic unit so that it is impossible now for the individual not to be conscious of the whole of the human race, and of our need of each other, and has created an economy of abundance.

At the same time its denial of relation between the private and the public life has made the mutual understanding of one individual or group by another increasingly more difficult.

The very worldly wisdom which has helped Catholicism to survive has hindered its development. While continuing to uphold and even intensifying its insistence upon unity of belief, it has always formulated its essential dogmas so as to admit of different interpretations suitable to different levels of intellectual understanding—a theologian's idea of the Resurrection of the Body is very different from that of an illiterate peasant—and to tolerate eccentricities like the cult of the Sacred Heart or the worship of local deities disguised as saints which satisfied eccentrics without impairing its central position. In consequence no other organisation has its range and variety, and though its political record has been consistently evil, and though its hierarchy is perhaps the most corrupt, none has produced more saints.

As a coarse generalisation one might say that Catholicism betrays the reason, Protestantism the heart. The former injures those who are capable of reasoning about the nature of the world, because it denies equality in intellectual inquiry and insists on authority. I have never met a Catholic intellectual—I exclude artists because artists never believe anything—who did not make me feel he was betraying his conscience.

But in admitting equality in worship, it allows the poor and uneducated, who take their beliefs for granted, the right to live by faith.

Protestantism, on the other hand, by admitting equality in reason, allows the intellectual to live by faith and be sceptical about belief, but denying equality in feeling, for it makes worship private and incommunicable, it forces the uneducated to live by crude uncivilised beliefs and moralities. The intellectual worships in private, the masses, rich or poor, are left with communal worship which is either dull or disgusting.

The whole complex of ideas which we call Romanticism is the attempt of Protestantism to find its own brand of Catholic unity, as the evil effects of separating the private and public life become apparent.

Romanticism says in effect: "Catholicism says only Unity is possible in this world; Protestantism that only Equality is possible. Both agree that the two are found together only in the next world, and that this world is ruled by fear. This is not good enough. Man cannot lead a double life: he desires unity and equality on this earth and to live by love not by fear. He can do this if he will trust the heart and distrust the reason. The Catholics believed in unity of reasoned belief, but the more men think, the more they disagree: the Protestants believed in Equality through reason, but Science has no love. Love is of the heart, of the body, for it is our physical lives that are similar and equal. Before Man began to think, there was unity and equality in this world. He can recover this if he will only trust his instinctive animal nature and abandon his pride of intellect."

In denying both the Catholic assertion that the physical world was intrinsically evil, and the Protestant assertion that it was not ruled by love, Romanticism took a great step forward. But it still believed in two Gods, the God of Love and the God of fear, only for the old dualism of the natural and supernatural worlds, it substituted a dualism of body and mind, heart and reason.

Because it lacked faith in the application of the law of love to human reason, while intending the reign of universal love on earth, it intensified materialism and group hatreds, for the reason is the power to relate our direct to our indirect experience, it is reason alone that makes it possible to love the brother whom we have not seen, and to love our enemies, because we understand their intention.

If the reason is evil, then we must go further than the Catholics who at least believed it was possible to think correctly, and must prevent its development altogether. The real enemy is the intellectual whatever he thinks. This prevention cannot be done by Catholic Sacraments, or Protestant reasoning but by direct physical action and the blind force of the human will.

The effects of Romanticism both for good and evil have been prodigious. It derives its dynamic power from its double faith, first in the possibility of realising Unity and Equality on earth, and secondly in the intrinsic goodness of the physical world. If its large-scale political influence has been almost wholly bad, since with faith only in emotion and personal relations, it had no equipment for organisation, and stimulated demagogy, and the wooliest kinds of humanitarianism from which the reaction into the worship of brutality and bureaucracy is now only too obvious, yet in social relations of a personal nature, sex relations, parenthood, education, athletics, its influence has been almost wholly good.

The Catholic historians are right who see the breaking away of the reformed churches as a tragedy. Had Erasmus rather than Luther triumphed, not only might we already have achieved a United States of Europe, but also a complete abandonment of dogmatic belief.

As it is, Catholicism, Protestantism, and Romanticism divide the truth between them. Each has and lacks something essential, so that none can either perish or triumph.

From the point of view of a just social order, Catholicism accepts social and economic inequality, but accompanies it by belief in the social responsibility of the superior for the inferior. The English political system, with its strongly marked class system and inequality of opportunity, but with its tradition of public service by the gentry as landlords, politicians, civil servants, etc., is the typical Catholic tradition.

Catholicism is correct in saying that men are not equal, but wrong in saying that inequality is a matter of birth, that the inferior necessarily beget the inferior.

Protestantism corrects the latter, but in asserting that men are in fact equal denies social responsibility. The

American political system shows both its virtues and defects.

Romanticism is right in asserting against them both the goodness of the material world, but wrong in denying against them both the goodness of reason.

Socialism has attempted to synthesise these three, to combine the Catholic faith in social responsibility and reason, the Protestant faith in equality and reason, and the Romantic faith in the physical world and emotion. By combining faith in reason and emotion it has been able to reverse the Romantic nostalgia for the past, and recover for the first time since Jesus the apocalyptic vision of history, to see history as moving in the direction of unity and equality. Yet it has failed and failed conspicuously and for one reason, because of the absolute division it makes between Past-Present "Pre-History" and the future conscious "History," a division as absolute as the Catholic division between this world and the next, the Protestant division between the private and the public life, and the Romantic division between the heart and the intellect.

No one should know better than the Marxists with their theory of the interpenetration of opposites, that nothing can be destroyed and that growth is continuous, that synthesis does not result from a liquidation of the thesis by the antithesis, yet they act as if this miracle were possible. They say in effect: "The material world of tomorrow will be ruled by love and the State will wither away. The material world of today is ruled by fear. Rule by fear, be politically realistic, and the Parousia will arrive."

Socialism is correct in saying that the world will inevitably become socialist, and that the actions of an individual can only either accelerate or retard that development, but in accepting the use of violence and hatred now, in believing that the laws which govern history today differ from those that will govern it tomorrow, they are doing the opposite of what they imagine: they are ranging themselves on the side of the retarders.

The effect of this error is already obvious. As the advent of the socialist order is further and further delayed, the masses lose faith in the apocalyptic vision of Socialism and keep only its faith in violence.

Fascism is Socialism that has lost faith in the future. Its slogan is: "Now or Never." In demanding a dictator, it is really returning to the early Christians' demand for the arrival of the Good Life on earth through a supernatural miracle.

Yet for all its horrors, Fascism has made one advance upon Socialism, and it owes its success to this. It appeals because it insists that all the individuals within a state have a common need of each other: and the fact that it denies this common need in the relations of one state and another does not alter that truth.

The Corporate State will be created but not by Fascism because you cannot make people love each other by flogging them till they do, and you cannot combine belief in the duty of the individual to the State with belief in the free struggle of nations for a place in the sun.

Democracy and Socialism have fought a losing battle with Fascism because the former are divided between their suspicion that only love and tolerance work, and their lack of faith in the possibility of employing them wholeheartedly: they are acting against their better judgement. The latter has all the sure judgement of the single-minded animal.

The dilemma that to fight Fascism you have to become fascist yourself is now pretty generally realised.

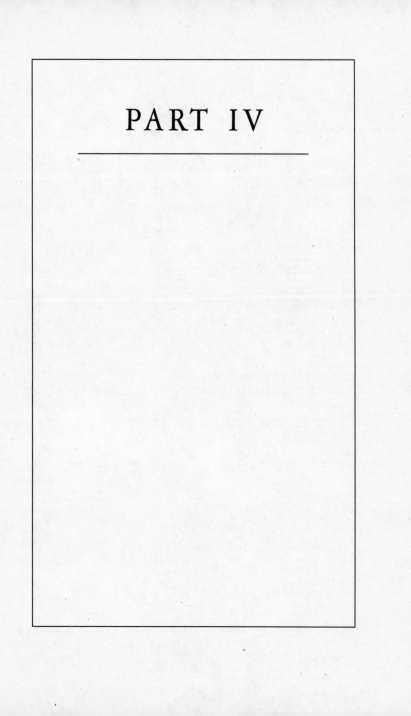

# PART IV

Q. Well, this all sounds very jolly and high-minded. But it is always suspicious when someone talks in terms of the universe, and historical epochs: we are particular people living in a particular world at a particular time. Let's get down then to particulars. First yourself. Frankly, do you believe in God and the supernatural?

A. If by God you mean a creator who is distinct from and independent of the creation, an omnipotent free-willing immaterial agent, no. I believe what, I suppose, everyone believes:

(1) That we are obliged to think that existence exists, that there is a universe of which the individual consciousness is only a part.

(2) That our human knowledge of existence obliges us to think of it as having essence, form, and motion but that these are intellectual abstractions from a manifold experience. There is no essence which is not organised in forms, and forms are always in motion: i.e., to speak of the separate existence of a form is an abstraction like speaking of a second in time.

(3) That our knowledge of existence organises it-self: we are obliged to see regularities or laws in the behaviour of existence, in the relation of forms in motion to each other.

(4) That we are obliged to think that truth is in-divisible and cannot conflict with itself.

If anyone chooses to call our knowledge of existence knowledge of God, to call Essence the Father, Form the Son, and Motion the Holy Ghost, I don't mind: Nomenclature is purely a matter of convenience. Mat-thew Arnold was wrong in saying that poetry was a substitute for religion, because religion is simply the way in which we live and poetry is not a substitute for life. But no religious dogma, i.e., no organisation of our emotions about life, can be anything but poetry, just as no one can regard a scientific theory any more as anything but a convenience, which one is no more asked to "believe" than one is asked to "believe" a po-etic statement.

(5) That our success as human beings whether in our emotional, intellectual, or material life is dependent upon

(a) The accuracy of our knowledge of these laws

(b) the conformity of our actions with our knowledge.

In addition I believe that our experience forces us to think the nature of the laws which govern the relations of forms is one which when described in terms of rela-tions between conscious human beings we call Love.

To this you may or may not agree: but I insist that

you apply the same test that you would apply to any other statement about the nature of existence, i.e., the empirical proof.

Your acceptance or rejection must be a matter of Faith, not Superstition. Neither for you nor for me can it be a dogmatic belief because our knowledge of the universe can never be complete.

As to the supernatural: again, if you mean a world governed by laws which bear no relation to the laws we know, I don't believe in it. I only believe that our knowledge is limited but capable of extension. On a question like survival after death, for example, I do not personally believe in it: but I should be prepared to do so if and when

> (a) Someone could convince me that the evidence of our senses oblige us to admit it
> (b) Our interpretation of this world and our interpretation of the next could be harmonised into one body of truth.

Q. Do you believe then in a Church of poetic Freethinkers?

A. No. I think that the Catholics and the Protestants were both right and both wrong. Worship *an und für sich* is not an action or a belief, but the state of mind necessary in order to do anything successfully whether by oneself or in association with others, i.e., a state of interest and love.

A church is simply any association of people with a common need and engaged on a common task.

The Catholics were right in saying that the Catholic Church must include the whole human race. It already does, but this is the result not of conversion but of exploration and trade: the world is already one place, and there is no longer any such thing as isolation.

But there are as many religious services as there are gatherings of two or more people to do something, and as various in character.

The Protestants were right in saying that what are commonly called religious exercises, i.e., actions the aim of which is the inducement of a state of worship, are private, not communal. There is no such thing as communal worship: communal actions are always directed to a specific end: the purpose of worship is to make communal action possible. The mistake of the Protestants was thinking that private worship could be successfully undertaken without consulting authorities. Private worship requires technique, and technique requires a teacher, if possible voluntarily chosen by the pupil. The real priest is the qualified private consultant in any field; his authority rests, however, not on his paper qualifications but his personal skill, his success in producing results.

It has always been a weakness of organised Christianity that its interest in a technique of worship has been concentrated on the development of a satisfactory liturgy. A technique of private meditation, contemplation, prayer, or whatever one likes to call it has never been made a professional tradition, but has remained uncorrelated and amateur, a series of isolated discoveries by individual mystics. This is serious because a technique, unlike a theory, can neither be written down nor learnt from a book, but has to be taught personally through a teacher-pupil relationship. Catholicism has been better in this respect than Protestantism: in the practice of Confession, for example, it has emphasised the need for proper qualification and skilled direction.

The failure of the one Protestant body which deserved to succeed, The Society of Friends, if due mainly to its adoption, in contradiction of its faith in Equality, of birthright membership, is also partly due to its lack of an adequate technique of private meditation. Valuable as the technique of a Quaker meeting is, so valuable that it is probably indispensable to the running of any kind of democratic organisation, the Friends overestimated the power of the group to cure the unintegrated individual. Though it would be an insult to compare them with the Oxford Groupers, they suffer a little from the same easy optimism; their faith in the Inner Light has not been sufficiently accompanied by scepticism as to their own readiness to accept it or powers to interpret it. While the Catholics overrate the capacity of the expert, and the Calvinists or writers like Kafka overemphasise the universal wickedness of man and his complete inability to know the truth, they are a valuable corrective to those who imagine that anyone whatever their condition can with a few quiet moments and a few prayers change their life and know the whole truth. Our fears and hatreds are not so easily banished.

In the East there has always been a better tradition

of private meditation, just because perhaps organised religion and political and social life had been so corrupt that for those who had reached a certain degree of consciousness public life was no longer possible.

In the West the recognition of the necessity for such a technique has developed via medicine rather than organised religion. The scientific study of man's material and physical life which began seriously after the Reformation has already arrived at the point where it finds that both the breakdown and the cure of the body are inseparable from the breakdown and cure of the mind, that there can be no successful active life without a trained contemplative life and vice versa. It is becoming more and more obvious that ordinary medicine, psychology, gymnastics and dietetics, Western Mysticism and Eastern Yoga are partial techniques with a common aim. Though they still continue either to be unaware of or to ignore each other, the relation of one technique to another is becoming more and more obvious.

As Western Europeans we are the only people with an intellectual tradition which is at once empirical and rational, i.e., one which forbids us to deny either evidence or the unity of truth and prevents us from being purely cranky Protestants or blindly orthodox Catholics, and it is therefore our task to synthesise these various pieces into a common ever-advancing technique.

Q. I conclude from all this that you have taken up Pacifism. This shocks me. In fact, I feel much as we once imagined one of us would feel if the other turned Roman Catholic.

A. Certainly my position forbids me to act as a combatant in any war. But if by pacificism you mean simply the refusal to bear arms, I have very little use for it. Nothing costs one less to do, for no one wants to do it. No social ostracism or imprisonment could possibly be as unpleasant as having to face a bayonet charge: personally I would rather face a firing squad.

History is the sum of individual actions present and past. A war is not produced out of a hat by a few politicians: it is the consequence of an infinite number of private acts of fear, violence, and hatred. To think that it is enough to refuse to be a soldier and that one can behave as one chooses as a private citizen, is to be quite willing to cause a war but only unwilling to suffer the consequences. I have more respect for Hitler.

Q. So you are going to settle down to the cultivation of your garden and your own soul while the world perishes?

A. No. The cultivation of the soul is certainly necessary, because without it one can only be ineffective in action. If you deny the effectiveness of violence it does not relieve you of the duty of political action, i.e., of action with other human beings; on the contrary, it makes action all the more imperative, for it forces you to admit that active evil is better than passive good. It does, however, dictate the kind of actions which you can do: it limits them to those which do not involve using violence or stimulating hatred, and these in their turn are of course limited by your own particular talents.

In the past in most places and today in some, social life may have been such that only the purely private life was possible without violence, but that is no longer true in the West. Even during a war, I think you must admit that there are a number of actions which are both non-violent and necessary, and enough to cover almost every kind of capacity. In peacetime there are still more. To justify an action to myself it must seem both non-violent and necessary: to justify it to others it is sufficient if they admit that it is necessary. Passivity is justifiable to neither.

Q. You are in fact opposed to revolution, though unlike the fascists you would express your opposition not by using counter-force but by peaceful (diplomatic) methods. In fact you would take sides with the fascists against the socialists but you would use other methods of attack. Let me remind you that you are a writer. If you wish to remain genuinely neutral in the fascist-communist conflict you will have to abstain from expressing your pacifist views because they are bound to injure whichever side you happen to be in closest contact with.

A. The problem for the writer of what to say and where and when to say it is certainly a very difficult one. If I wished to be neutral you are right in saying that I should have to abstain from expressing my views. My justification for speaking is precisely because I believe Socialism to be right but believe the theory and practice of revolution to be wrong in the sense that I do not believe it will conquer Fascism and establish Socialism. I am therefore bound to try and convince socialists that they are wrong about revolution.

On the other hand I recognise that it is only too easy to make men accept the negative side of anything one says, in this case, to persuade them to give up revolutionary action, without putting anything in its place, and the negative is always harmful.

For instance, I think that all meetings of protest, whether of socialists against fascist atrocities or of pacifists against war, are harmful: a meeting must have a specific and positive purpose, to decide on a course of action, to collect money, to enjoy oneself, etc.

As a writer one must distinguish between art and propaganda. I call propaganda a statement which can be understood intellectually without being understood emotionally, i.e., confirmed by one's own experience: to write it is to ignore the fact that different people are at different stages of development.

Direct statement like all these remarks can only be used in an effort to convince those whom, like yourself, I know personally, or to clarify the thinking of those who already agree with me.

To others one must talk in parables; one must use as one's artistic subject matter material where the truth of non-violence convinces without offending, and let them extend the conclusion to other fields for themselves. Under certain circumstances, like actual wartime, it may well be that it is unwise to publish anything, and better to concentrate upon actions which have nothing to do with writing.

Q. You don't think that revolution will ever work out right. Of course it won't. But—as Forster says—"Life won't work out." Pacifism deals always in mystical absolutes. War is evil: therefore all wars at all periods of history are equally evil, no matter whether they result in ten hundred or ten million casualties, whether they lead to a hundred years of reaction or make possible a cultural renaissance. War is evil: therefore the Chinese and Japanese governments, since both are at war, are equally wicked—and whichever side wins the war, the result will be absolutely evil. What half-baked trash it is: first you postulate a rigid absolute and call it "Good"; then you postulate another and call it "Evil"; and then you assert quite logically that one can't come out of the other. But reality has nothing to do with absolute Good and Evil. In the Marxist view there are two kinds of war—the reactionary and the progressive. The war of 1914 was an example of the first, and the war of China against Japan is an example of the second. Whenever an oppressed class or nation is fighting against its oppressor there you have a just war, a war in which victory for the oppressed will be of greater benefit to the human race than victory for the oppressor.

If you say that the oppressed can never improve

their condition by fighting I answer that we are talking totally different languages.

You know that I loathe violence and shall make a very bad revolutionary, but I recognise that this is a weakness and I don't try to justify it.

A. I agree with every word of what you say, but then I never said anything different. Of course if the effects of war were evil in an absolute sense the human race would long ago have disappeared. Where I disagree with you is when you deny that life will work out. This seems to me to be contrary to the Marxism which you profess. The keynote of Marxism is surely that history has moved and is moving in a certain direction despite the efforts of individuals or classes to stop or deflect it: in other words, that life is working out. Perfection is certainly, if you like, a non-existent mystical absolute, but Marxism teaches that historical development is asymptotic to perfection. Its line isn't straight: it wiggles and makes spirals, but its general direction is perfectly clear.

Of course it matters whether the Chinese win or the Japanese: of course the oppressed can improve their condition by successful revolt: but even if the Chinese lose, or the oppressed are suppressed: it does not mean the end of progress, only that its rate of development is slower than it would have been if the Chinese or the oppressed had won. If war could have been avoided it would have been better still. If victory or defeat were absolute in their results, and if there were no acts of resistance except violent ones: i.e., if non-violent acts had no historical effects, refusal to fight would be indefensible.

You say that your loathing of violence is an unjustifiable weakness? Why? Because you imagine that this loathing is mere squeamishness, a dislike of doing something necessary just because it is unpleasant? If you imagine this, I think you deceive yourself. When it comes to hurting other people whom we don't know personally, particularly if one can do it from a safe distance, most of us are not as squeamish as we like to think. People were shocked when Mussolini's son said what fun it was dropping bombs on Abyssinian villages, but nine out of ten people, and I include myself among the nine, would feel exactly the same. If they couldn't fire back, I should enjoy potting at distant Germans as much as I enjoy potting at rabbits.

At close quarters it is another matter. One is shocked when one sees mangled air-raid victims and hears the weeping of the bereaved, because one puts oneself in their place. The emotional basis for hatred of violence is self-love; its intellectual basis is self-knowledge. One hates having violence done to oneself, and one knows that even if for the moment one is forced by it to obey another, its effect is to make one neither forget nor forgive, but to bide one's time for revenge. You know quite well what you would think of the headmaster who while beating you says: "This hurts me more than it hurts you." When you say you loathe violence you are confessing that, as it is impossible for anyone to believe that violence will do them any good, you have doubts as to whether violence is an effective as your leaders tell you.

Your doubts may be mistaken, but doubts must be solved: to wish them away by calling them unjustifiable weakness is dishonest.

Q. I see that you believe that violence always punishes itself. This is false. "Those that take the sword shall perish by the sword" is far nearer the truth. But violence is not always punished even by somebody else's violence, and the majority of those that take the sword do not perish by the sword. The majority of the soldiers who fought in the 1914 war survived it, and very few generals do not die in bed.

A. I entirely agree with your last sentence, but I should have thought that the state of the world today was sufficient proof that the violence of 1914 incurred a punishment. The trouble about violence is that most of the punishment falls on the innocent. That is why, even if you imagine you are fighting for the noblest of ends, the knowledge that it is more your children than yourself who will have to pay for your violence, that should make you hesitate.

Q. In condemning violence you are falling into that old fallacy of rigidly separating Means and Ends. Means condition ends and vice versa. Is it bad to cut a man's flesh with a knife? Yes, if you mean to wound him. No, if you are incising an abscess.

A. Means are conditioned by ends and knowledge. For example, in conducting a successful experiment I must have an end, say, the making of sodium chloride, and I must know something about the laws of chemical combination. If I use the wrong means, if I mix copper and nitric acid, I shall fail in achieving my end. I can, however, even if I start with these materials produce sodium chloride in the end after a series of experiments.

The use of violence to achieve socialism seems to me to resemble the experiments of an unskillful chemist.

As to your medical analogy, I am surprised at you of all people using the Body-Politic argument which I always thought was the property of the fascists. You hardly need me to tell you that the state is an aggregate of conscious individuals and the body a single consciousness; that the pus cells do not suffer, remember, and hate like human beings, nor have they relatives, and that the decision to operate in the case of society is made and the decision carried out not by a single transcendent consciousness but by other cells who presume to decide what tissue is healthy and what is not, so that the effect of surgery is very different from the effect of revolution. (Incidentally, with every advance in medical knowledge distrust of surgery grows.)

The nearest comparison would be that social violence is like curing a man of cancer by operation and giving him neurasthenia instead, which in its turn is cured by malaria and so on.

Q. You keep evading the real political issue. Of course it is better that the oppressed should obtain their freedom without war if they can, but you know as well as I that they can't. Are you seriously suggesting that the Abyssinians or the Spanish Loyalists should have simply let the Italians and Franco take power without a struggle?

A. It is you who are going in for mystical absolutes now. History is never a matter of "should" in an absolute sense. As I said before, history at any given moment is the sum of all the actions being done. What these actions are depends upon their intention, and the agent's knowledge of how best to realise his particular intention, and both intention and knowledge depend upon his past actions and those of others living and dead. "Political," i.e., the mass action of a class or a nation, is roughly in accordance with the average intention and knowledge of the individuals who make up that class or nation; it can be better or worse than the average but not by very much. The degree of variation from the norm can be greater in countries where there is a dictator or an unchallenged ruling class than in a democratic country, but the independence in action of the politician from the will of the majority is getting less and less every year. No dictator could exist with the secret police alone and without propaganda.

It is unrealistic nonsense to ask whether the Abyssinians or the Spanish Loyalists or the Chinese should or should not have resisted, or for that matter whether the Italians or the Rebels or the Japanese should have attacked. These wars have occurred because the majority of people on both sides want certain things and believe—whether or no they have been tricked into believing it is beside the point—that these can only be obtained by violence.

If the whole Abyssinian or the Chinese people, or the majority of them, had reached such a degree of understanding that they all refused to use violence, there would be no war because the same thing would have happened in the countries of the aggressors. It is impossible for one part of the world to develop so much more rapidly than another that a situation could arise where one nation was non-violent and another violent; the world is now too interrelated.

The only moral judgement one is justified in making about the political behaviour of a nation or class is the same one that can be made about an individual: "Is it acting in accordance with its fullest knowledge of how to achieve its ends?—i.e., the fullest extent in the first case of the average knowledge."

But nations and classes are not idealist entities, they are aggregates of individuals. The average level of consciousness which elects political leaders and dictates political action depends on the consciousness of every individual: an increase or distortion in a single individual raises or lowers, however slightly, that average. The effect of the individual upon politics is slight but real, and the effect is very little connected with his interest or lack of interest in politics, since for most people politics are a very small part of their life, and their political effect is the sum total of their acts.

The greater part of your own political effect, for instance, does not come from the specifically political work you do but from your everyday working and private life, the hours you spend teaching, the money you spend in shops, buses, cinemas, etc.

What is required of an individual is that he shall try always to increase his knowledge of how to act effectively and try always not to act contrary to his knowledge. Only in that way is it possible to raise the average level of the mass and so to improve political action.

Q. You mean all politics is a dirty game and should be left to scoundrels. You join the gang who say that the world will only be saved by a change of heart. Is that it?

A. No. I only say that today politicians depend upon the support of the masses, and in consequence are representatives of the average man of their country and time, sometimes a bit better, sometimes a bit worse. If they were much better or much worse they would not succeed, because they would never be accepted by the masses. It has always been the dream of philosophers that one could have government by the Best People, and the dream has never come true, because you cannot change any human being in a moment. If you have democratic election, the Best People are not chosen. If those who believe that they are the Best People, even if they really are, seize power, they find themselves forced to become tyrants, because they are so far above the average that the average neither understands nor likes them.

This means that if you are much above the average in understanding and sensibility you will probably not be able to do much politically in the narrow sense of that word, because you will very soon find yourself forced to do things in which you don't fully believe, which means that in practice you will fail, for it is impossible to do anything successfully unless one believes completely in what one is doing. You admit this when you say that your hatred of violence will make you a bad revolutionary.

I certainly don't think that the world will be saved only by a change of heart. I believe that the world will be saved though, that historical development through every channel, wars, technology, psychology, etc., etc., will compel a change of heart, that both our mistakes and our successes increase our understanding, the latter directly, the former indirectly by inducing another kind of mistake. And I know that what is popularly called politics is only a tiny part of what causes history to move.

I think that your attitude, the division you make between what you call your private life and what you call politics, is due firstly to a lack of faith in the direction of historical movement towards Socialism, a faith which as a Marxist you have no right to lack, and secondly an overestimation of the historical effect of so-called political action, and an underestimation of the historical effect of the so-called private life, which as a matter of fact is by far the largest part of history, as the Marxist materialist approach has proved. You are at once too conceited and too humble. Your conceit about the effect of your "political" life prevents you from seeing that Hitler because of the greater number of people whom he affects is doing more, indirectly and in spite of himself, to bring about Socialism than your political acts can ever do.

Your humility about your "private" life prevents you from seeing that all the hundreds of acts which you and millions of others do every day which are socialist, i.e., in which you unite thought and intention and treat others with love and as equals, are making history and defeating Hitler, or rather making the world impossible for Hitlers.

I am not suggesting that you should be negative, only that you should concentrate on those actions in which you fully believe, i.e., in which you can succeed. What those are you must decide for yourself. There will be violence and wars for many many years to come, and they will accomplish something, but you must leave their conduct to those who sincerely believe in them.

Q. Then you don't believe in political parties or party discipline?

A. Not much. Government in every economically advanced country is becoming increasingly one party, i.e., whatever their names, their programmes cannot differ very radically from each other, for they have to carry the masses with them. Both industrialism and general education have so complicated the class structure that no party can succeed by trying to satisfy the interests of a single element in society, whether it be the unemployed or the Oil Companies. The main political struggle today is the inside struggle for control of a party between the more intelligent and sensitive and the less.

In the democratic countries nothing is doing more to discredit democracy than party discipline. The man-in-the-street is not such a fool as to be taken in when he sees Government supporters voting for measures of which he knows that they are critical, or Opposition members voting against measures which, were they in power, they would have to carry through.

And I fancy that under a dictatorship the reverse is true: party discipline and inability to criticise discredits dictatorship.

Q. Are you prepared to have anything to do with politics in the strict sense?

A. For myself personally there are other things that interest me more and for which I think I am more suited. But that is purely personal. I certainly think it extremely important that people should take part in politics, provided that they do something constructive, municipal politics for example, or social anthropology, finding out what the electorate are really like, or relief work or ferreting out unpleasant suppressed facts or what have you. The kind of politics which seems to me very dangerous is pure oppositionism. Opposition and criticism is necessary and valuable, but the Left spends far too much time in my opinion in protest meetings, and revivalist anti-fascist services, a mistake which will cost them dear, I'm afraid, with the electorate.

Q. But political parties do in fact exist. Do you think it doesn't matter which you support or vote for?

A. Yes, I do think it matters, but the choice depends on the particular election. There are four factors to take into consideration:
    (1) The general nature of the party programme.
    (2) One's estimation of the power of the party, if successful, to realise it.
    (3) The character and capacity of the party leaders.
    (4) The character and capacity of the local candidate.
In casting my vote I would put the order of importance of these as 3-1-2-4.